HIERARCHY OF RECOVERY

HIERARCHY OF RECOVERY

From Abstinence to Self-Actualization

Robert S. Helgoe, Ph.D.

Hazelden
Center City, Minnesota 55012-0176

1-800-328-0094
1-651-213-4590 (Fax)
www.hazelden.org

Library of Congress Cataloging-in-Publication Data
    Helgoe, Robert S., 1943 -
        Hierarchy of recovery : from abstinence to self-actualization /
        Robert S. Helgoe.—2nd ed.
            p. cm.
    Previously published as: Recovery: a pull from the source. Selah, Wash. :
        Sundown M Foundation, c1989.
            ISBN 1-56838-884-5 (pbk.)
    1. Addicts—Rehabilitation. 2. Self-actualization (Psychology)
    3. Substance abuse—Treatment.
    I. Helgoe, Robert S., 1943- Recovery. II. Title.

RC564 .H45 2002
616.86'03—dc21

                                                                2002068542

06 05 04 03   6 5 4 3 2

Cover design by David Spohn
Interior design and typesetting by Kinne Design

CONTENTS

PREFACE

This book is written primarily for chemical dependency counselors and students who are looking for ideas and methods to assess and evaluate the recovery of alcoholic and addicted patients. As you read this book, please remember that alcoholism and chemical addictions are diseases. What may seem to be the "psychologizing" of recovery is not meant to imply that the origin of the disease or the disease itself need psychologizing to explain them. They do not. However, the recovery process, once the addiction is arrested, deserves more attention from the best psychology available, and that is what this book does, especially in chapter 5 (based on Abraham Maslow's powerful ideas) and chapter 7 (based on the wisdom of Alcoholics Anonymous).

The overall goal of this book is to promote further thinking and discussion on recovery and to include patients in this discussion. The accompanying facilitator's guide and client workbook are additional tools to promote this discussion. The facilitator's guide provides counselors with suggestions on how to use the tracking measures that are introduced in this book: the AAA Profile, the Promises Checklist, and Maslow's hierarchy. The client workbook provides the corresponding set of recovery-oriented tools for the recovering person's use.

ACKNOWLEDGMENTS

I want to thank the former Director of Sundown M Ranch, Pierre Brown, and the current Director, Scott Munson, for their support of this work.

Richard Solly, editor at Hazelden, has been instrumental in fashioning the scope and clarity of the book.

Susan Tinker and Michele Koci, administrators at Skagit Valley College, have been enthusiastic supporters of this and other projects of mine, and I appreciate their continued reinforcement.

My colleagues Jean Matthews, Bob Malphrus, Mike Doran, Janice Condrin, Rob Martin, Janet Walthew, Alan Erickson, and Linda Grant have influenced the contents and spirit of the book in countless ways. They are inspiring examples of the sort of self-actualizing people I write about.

To MaryDell Harrison I give special thanks for times of thinking and laughing and envisioning which are part of the Pull in my life.

And to my daughter Katie: thanks for being there when the Light shines.

INTRODUCTION

Professionals in the field of chemical dependency have not reached a consensus on how to define or measure recovery from alcoholism and other drug addictions. While norms of diagnosing and treating these conditions have been established, a standard on gauging whether treatment is working effectively and how to document recovery does not yet exist.

In 1999 I went to Boston for a working conference on treatment effectiveness and outcomes, including what to measure, sponsored by the Commission on Accreditation of Rehabilitation Facilities (CARF), an organization which accredits chemical dependency treatment facilities, as well as other types of agencies. The three main indexes of the CARF criteria for accreditation concern the treatment outcome factors of effectiveness, efficiency, and satisfaction. The various ways to measure these, however, were still in development. Even when fully researched and manualized, there is the expectation that such measures and criteria will improve and yet be flexible enough to accommodate new developments in treatment practices, client populations, reporting requirements, and how treatment is paid for. CARF, like most accrediting bodies, is eager to see the field give deeper attention to these concerns from an internal motivation to improve treatment than from an external pressure to comply with imposed outside standards.

My interest extends beyond the treatment outcome measures referred to above into what can be called posttreatment recovery. I do not see treatment as an end in itself. Treatment-related criteria of progress are not necessarily reflective of the changes required for long-term recovery. Recovery and Twelve Step programs are not adjuncts to facilitate treatment, but the other way around.

For example, much of the professional recovery literature addresses relapse prevention as the main entry into the broader topic of recovery. Many relapse prevention models (for example, Gorski 1989) present recovery as a series of tasks, efforts, and activities that the patient must complete in order to prevent relapse or reversal of progress. Most relapse prevention programs take place in a treatment setting often accompanying or shortly following primary treatment. Facilitators are treatment or prevention specialists.

But what keeps people going in recovery after they are no longer "patients"? Why make self-inventories, disclose secrets, make amends, and go to meetings not connected to a treatment facility? Are those activities ends in themselves or are they means to some other end? And what could *that* end be?

Initially, the patient has pragmatic reasons for staying sober: "Because if I don't, the judge will send me to jail," or "I was going to die if I kept going the way I was. Now I have a chance." As people gain more time in recovery, their motivation eventually changes and becomes tied to internal experiences and personal incentives: "I want to stop just fooling around and lead a full life," or "My friend is happy, joyous, and free and I want that too." Yet few models of relapse prevention ask the patient whether those motivational changes are happening, and even when the patient says they are, it is treated with suspicion and warnings about self-deception. Instead, the inquiries and record keeping of the professional counselor are tied to the patient's *initial* reasons for entering treatment: "Have you been to court yet?" "Did you pay your rent?" "Did you go to three meetings this week?" "Have you been practicing the three coping skills you learned last week?"

The goals of most chemical dependency treatment programs are to (1) stabilize the patient, (2) weaken and examine denial, and (3) introduce a recovery program. All of these goals are considered supportive of the overarching goal of achieving and maintaining abstinence. Once abstinent, patients are expected to assume more and more responsibility for themselves. This may include not fighting, paying the rent, not blaming, following directions, learning the rules, going to meetings, learning coping skills, solving problems, getting the support of a recovery group, learning to make responsible choices, functioning effectively socially, establishing stable relationships, learning more coping skills, solving or complying with legal issues, getting a job, completing the treatment plan, and using all those coping skills.[1] Why shouldn't these goals be the criteria used to measure recovery, in addition to the basic and essential criterion of abstinence?

The reason is simple: such goals do not describe who every recovering person wants to become as he or she gains more time in recovery. They are not the marks of a meaningful life. Although the above agenda makes sense during treatment, none of the goals listed are ends in themselves. These accomplishments are not what a person would have inscribed on his or her headstone; they're not what anyone wants to be remembered for. Yet, they are steps toward bigger goals. Both are important in recovery. But rather than focus solely on the elementary steps of early recovery, we should also ask what the person ultimately wants, and is the patient, the recovering person, getting it?

Recovery consists of a series of levels, or phases, that build upon each other, starting with abstinence. This book will present a four-element plan to both define and assess recovery as a progressive, dynamic process. Here are the steps in that plan:

1. Reveal a mixed consensus on what constitutes recovery, because there are two distinct phases in the recovery process: an initial phase and a long-term phase. Most models of recovery address only the initial phase, which explains why most professionals list only treatment goals as criteria for recovery. However, the literature of Alcoholics Anonymous (AA) and other sources address both phases of recovery, initial and long-term, and suggest criteria quite different from the above.

2. Argue that the literature of Alcoholics Anonymous contains both the long-term goals of recovery, in the form of the Promises, and a process leading to them revealed and measured by a simple test called the AAA Profile.

3. Show how the goals and outcomes in Alcoholics Anonymous are not only compatible with the concepts of Self-Actualization psychology, but are similar to the goals, values, and characteristics of self-actualizing persons.

4. Present an inventory, in the form of a checklist, that measures the degree to which these goals are being realized by people in treatment and recovery and which may provide a common set of criteria that both counselors and clients can agree to use as markers to evaluate recovery progress.

The American Heritage Dictionary lists several definitions for the word *recovery*, the first is, *the getting back of something lost*. In the model of recovery being offered here, the "something lost" is the patient's ability to be self-actualizing. The dictionary offers the origin of the term *assessment*, which comes from the Latin *ad*, near or next to, plus *sedere*, to sit or place. That is, to compare. This is what patients and counselors are doing in treatment: comparing what is present at the moment to what had come before, to what has been lost, and to what is expected to lie ahead. This activity is always taking place. This book suggests a way to examine that process more systematically.

1

RECOVERY:
BY WHAT CRITERIA?

"How do you as a counselor know when people are making progress in their treatment, and how do you make a prognosis about that person's future recovery? How should recovery be measured?" These are questions that I pass on to you, the reader, having had them asked of me when I was director and a counselor in the San Juan Community Alcohol Center, Friday Harbor, Washington. The person asking the questions was a judge, to whom I had been regularly sending reports on progress and prognosis of patients referred by the court, usually people whose alcoholism had produced DWI arrests. The judge wanted to know what my "clinical judgment" was based on. At the time, I had answers which satisfied the judge but which left me questioning the validity of my judgment. Did I use the same standards for all patients? Was I employing treatment response criteria and recovery benchmarks that would stand up to my own scrutiny, much less that of others? I wasn't sure. I didn't have anything on my desk that I invariably consulted in composing progress updates, other than the patient file. But progress compared with what? Each patient's treatment plan established a list of obligations, such as participating in individual and group sessions, attending outside AA meetings, completing written work, and, of course, abstaining from alcohol and other psychoactive drugs. So I was able to document the patient's compliance with a treatment plan. This turned out to be the most objective information I could offer the judge. The rest of it—the individually centered clinical impression I had of the patient—was based on something else. It bothered me that I couldn't pin down that "something else." I decided to share the problem.

In August 1986, I asked people attending a conference on alcoholism and recovery to list three ways they thought recovery could be measured. Of the eighty-one people in the group, thirty-eight were chemical dependency counselors certified by the Washington State Chemical Dependency Certification Board and forty-three were students, allied professionals, or interested parties. I posed this scenario to the group: "Assume you are working with a client who has been through primary treatment for alcoholism, has been continuously abstinent for one year, and you want to know how well he has 'progressed in recovery.' I want you to list the three most significant objective or measurable criteria that you would use to evaluate that person's recovery." I gave them ten minutes. Nearly everyone took the full time allowed, and all bent to the task with concentration. It did not appear to be easy.

This exercise certainly was not a sound research protocol, but it was instructive. Table 1 presents the results (Helgoe 1986).

The eighty-one respondents each listed three criteria for a total of 234, which I sorted into eighteen categories, listed in order of decreasing frequency in table 1. The frequency of each category's inclusion as a criterion is indicated in the second column. Columns three and four show the frequency broken down by the two groups of respondents, the certified alcoholism counselors (CAC) versus the rest of the audience, the non-CAC group.

TABLE 1

Response Categories for Recovery Criteria

RESPONSE CATEGORY	N = 81 x 3 TOTAL (234)	n = 38 CAC	n = 43 non-CAC
1. Stable support / AA connected	40	22	18
2. Self-responsible choices	24	13	11
3. Social functioning	20	9	11
4. Stable relationships / family	20	6	14
5. Contentment / serene feelings	15	6	9
6. Acceptance / attitude change	15	4	11
7. Following Tx / therapy plan	14	4	10
8. Long-term goals / life style	13	8	5
9. Employment / financial stability	12	6	6
10. Self-esteem	11	5	6
11. Physical appearance	8	3	5
12. Spiritual connection	7	4	3
13. Problem solving skills	7	4	3
14. Enjoying life / sense of wellness	5	4	1
15. Coping skills for stress	5	3	2
16. Absence of desire to drink	5	2	3
17. Legal status	2	1	1
18. Humor / laughter	1	0	1
Unclassifiable / unreadable	10	5	5

The results (see table 1) demonstrated a lack of consensus on what criteria indicate recovery beyond simple abstinence. I was surprised at how few of the criteria that I personally believed measured recovery were listed. For example, only fifteen people (six CACs and nine non-CACs) mentioned "serenity" as a criterion they would look for (category 5) and only five mentioned "enjoying life." Forty persons (about half of the total group) mentioned category 1, having a stable support group or an AA connection. Except for categories 4 and 6, little difference existed between the responses of the certified counselors and that of others in the group.

From this survey, I concluded that people consider what patients *should* be doing to stay sober as a yardstick for evaluating their recovery. Five of the six most frequently given criteria demonstrate the thinking that recovering people should attend support groups, make responsible choices, and so forth. In other words, they follow the *treatment plan.*

Effective Treatment Plans

But what if the treatment plan itself is problematic? Consider an analogy of a patient being treated for the disease of diabetes. The patient's treatment plan calls for careful monitoring and control of blood sugar levels, regular laboratory blood analysis of glycosylated hemoglobin levels, frequent checks for foot and eye health, and so on. Two similar diabetics are following the same treatment plan yet have remarkably different problems and prognoses. One is showing dangerous blood sugar levels, has retinal problems, and feels miserable, whereas the other is doing "just fine" on all measures. The difference between them is not whether they are following the treatment plan (both are), but whether the treatment plan is helping them. The treatment plan for one patient needs to be adjusted because it's ineffective. The patient's failing health reveals this.

In the chemical dependency field, how do we know when a patient's treatment plan is not working? How does the patient know? What signs and symptoms of recovery, apart from the treatment plan, do we need to monitor in order to know if the plan should be changed?

The type of criteria with which I and most counselors

were familiar, as seen in table 1, measure compliance with a plan and the patient's progress in doing certain things: going to meetings, making responsible choices, and having a support group. These are not long-term goals or ends in themselves. They are all means to an end. In later recovery, however, end goals themselves should become the criteria each client uses to gauge whether his or her recovery is just average, good, or excellent. The goals of recovery shift as the client progresses from early- to long-term recovery, from simply attending meetings to gaining the benefits of such attendance. Is the person happier? Does the person feel he or she has a meaningful life?

The diversity of opinion in table 1 represents a mixture of short- and long-term goals,[1] means and ends, work and payoff, and efforts and results. *If* one develops more self-responsibility (category 2), *then* one might have more self-esteem (category 10). However, great self-esteem is not an end in itself. According to Abraham Maslow, whose concepts are discussed in chapter 5, self-esteem is a stepping-stone to a higher goal. As clients gain time in recovery, abstinence from alcohol and other drugs shifts from being a primary goal to becoming a means to something greater. To be sure, abstinence is necessary for recovery and is a miraculous achievement for some, but abstinence alone is not a *sufficient* condition for enjoying life, as chapter 3 will assert.

The question I began this section with needs to be rephrased: how can counselors more confidently estimate their patients' status in the recovery process? I have an answer. Counselors need to use criteria within a model of recovery that makes sense within a theory of human behavior that is understandable and useful to chemical dependency counselors and their patients. To do that, we either step outside the treatment plan or incorporate these elements into the plan itself.

A New Model

I offer a two-phase model of the recovery process (the Push-Pull model) and a model of how change takes place (AAA cycle), as well as a set of measures of both the process and outcomes of that change (AAA Profile, Promises Checklist, and two measures of change during treatment called the modified-GAF scores), and a theory of human behavior/motivation (Maslow) to bundle it all up in. Fortunately, all of this can be incorporated into existing treatment regimens without loss of momentum or time. For people in recovery, whether they are in treatment or not, this book may alert them to what to look for, prepare for, and ask for.

This book and these tools are offered not because the addictions treatment field is in shambles or not working well. On the contrary, treatment programs are doing remarkably well in arresting addictions and promoting recovery. Convincing others outside of the field that treatment works is made easier when we utilize tools like the *American Society of Addiction Medicine's Patient Placement Criteria (ASAM PPC)* and *DSM (Diagnostic and Statistical Manual of the American Psychiatric Association)* diagnostic protocols. Those tools enhance treatment and demonstrate that the field uses research-based and valid instruments respected by professionals. This book is motivated by a desire to make recovery from addictions more understandable and more easily measured, and ultimately to enhance the personal experience of it.

2

EARLY RECOVERY ASSESSMENT

Early recovery is a phase in which the first effects of treatment are realized. Researchers looking at this phase sometimes characterize their work as investigations of treatment effectiveness rather than as studies of a recovery process. This implies a cause-effect relationship: when we do this to the patient, the effect is such and such. (Later chapters will further distinguish between treatment variables and recovery variables, and assert that the recovery process begins to take on a "life of its own" apart from treatment outcomes.) To be sure, the effects of treatment and the early signs of recovery overlap, but they are not identical.

This chapter provides a summary of select studies on treatment effectiveness. Out of the vast recovery literature, these studies have been selected because they illustrate what happens when a person stops using addictive drugs and starts healing, and how we're aware of and measure that progress.

In an early review by Gibbs and Flanagan (1977, 1, 137), only two outcome measures were used: degree of abstinence and "social adjustment as measured on some indicator of social competence, e.g., employment record, marital stability." The researchers reviewed scores of studies investigating the link between certain markers, or "indicators" (such as birth order, MMPI score, Wechsler IQ, self-referral), and outcome of treatment as defined by the two previously named criteria. It was surprising how few indicators predicted "success" on either of the two criteria (none of the markers noted above predicted anything of clinical interest in the studies reviewed by Gibbs and Flanagan).

Sanchez-Craig (1988) conducted a review of predictive variables and a general critique of treatment-outcome research methodology. Her review, however, had an explicitly stated orientation toward treatment effectiveness and an implicit definition of recovery: "The principal objective of all alcoholism treatment programs is to reduce the level of drinking of their clients" (p. 60). That is, total abstinence was not a criterion or baseline for using other indexes of treatment effectiveness in studies reviewed by Sanchez-Craig. Although recovery begins with abstinence—total abstinence, not just a reduction—something must take the place of drinking for recovery to progress. The reviews by Gibbs and Flanagan and Sanchez-Craig did not indicate what that "something" is. Nor did they hold out much confidence in researchers' ability to define it.

Treatment Progress and Recovery

Some people mark their recovery from the moment of their last drink or dose, while others use the breaking of denial—one of the main tasks of primary treatment—as their marker. In either case, the first signs and symptoms of recovery are paradoxically often *new disorders*. Recovery starts when the client experiences new distress but no longer uses chemicals to deal with the discomfort.

Following is a discussion of several instruments used to measure recovery; we will look at their ability to detect the initial appearance and subsequent fate of a variety of negative indicators. A negative indicator is any sign or symptom that is a problem to either the client or the treatment staff. The reduction of the number, intensity, or duration of negative indicators is assumed to reveal progress in treatment. However, positive indicators do not necessarily appear when negative indicators dissipate (unless the positive indicators are measured just as directly as the negative ones and they are perfectly inversely correlated). In short, detecting the rate at which problems disappear is not the same as measuring positive recovery, though the former is a popular approach because more is known about measuring and confronting negative markers than positive markers, at least in early treatment. Documenting diminishing problems is done primarily in the early phases of treatment and recovery, followed later by attention to the attractions of long-term recovery. The early phase receives the most attention because this is the phase where most professionals are involved.

Several instruments have appeared in response to the need to develop standardized or more systematic evaluation of treatment readiness, response, and disposition toward recovery.

RAATE

Mee-Lee (1988) constructed an inventory called the Recovery Attitude and Treatment Evaluator (RAATE) that assesses five dimensions of inpatient client disposition:

1. degree of resistance to treatment;
2. degree of resistance to continuing care;
3. acuity of biomedical problems;
4. acuity of psychiatric problems; and,
5. extent of social/family problems unsupportive to recovery.

These measures later became key features of the *American Society of Addiction Medicine's Patient Placement*

Criteria (PPC), which Mee-Lee and others designed (Mee-Lee et al. 2001) to aid the accurate and appropriate evaluation and placement of clients into treatment settings. Clinical staff or assessment personnel, rather than the patient, answer the RAATE questions about the patient. This strategy is to provide for greater comparability of counselor's assessments across treatment settings, different client populations, and for researching treatment outcomes.

The RAATE and its descendant PPC are problem-oriented. With few exceptions, the RAATE questions concern problematic issues that the counselor can identify in the patient. None of the questions (which may be asked of the patient's attitudes or behaviors several times over the course of treatment) address what the patient is doing well. Instead, they relate to the patient's problems.

The tests are useful if recovery is defined solely as identifying problems and learning to cope with, master, endure, or banish them without turning to alcohol, drugs, and dependent behavior. In this case, recovery consists of minimizing the number of *negative* indicators, which is what the RAATE scales detect.

BESS

An inventory developed by Blum, et al., (1987), called the Behavioral, Emotional, Spiritual, and Social (BESS) Score, assists in measuring either negative or positive responses to treatment modalities. Like RAATE, BESS measures changes in patient attitude and behavior as perceived by the counselor; but unlike RAATE, BESS scores can change to reflect not just the lessening of aggravating conditions, but the acquisition of new, healthy experiences. The BESS score is composed of sub-scores, such as the patient's self-image, compliance, anger, cooperation, group participation, belief in

God, and general attitude in treatment. BESS is the forerunner of what has become known as the Strength Model of counseling and has influenced Motivational Interviewing (see, for example, Miller and Rollnick 1999).

Unfortunately, the BESS scale is a subjective clinical measure, was not standardized on a large treatment population for general use, and was too narrow in scope to cover the range of treatment options that became available in the 1990s. Instead, the *ASAM Patient Placement Criteria* (*PPC-2R*, Mee-Lee et al. 2001) are presently the best guidelines the profession has for valid assessment, referral, and monitoring of patient treatment.

An excellent guide for the use of these tools is found in Coughlin, Anderson, and Kimbro (1999). They note that the *PPC* is not intended to stand alone as a standard of treatment for individuals. The *PPC* allows the use of a combination of objective criteria and subjective professional judgment. Using the *PPC*, monitoring the patient in treatment proceeds with reference to the six dimensions of the placement criteria themselves, the same factors that determined the most suitable level of treatment initially. If the patient shows notable change in any of the circumstances, a change in level of treatment may be advised. The dimensions are

1. intoxication and/or withdrawal potential;
2. biomedical conditions and complications;
3. emotional, behavioral, or cognitive conditions;
4. readiness to change;
5. relapse or continued use potential; and
6. recovery environment.

These broad categories need to be tracked, but the *PPC* offers no specific tools or measures to do so. Instead, clinical observations relevant to the six dimensions are noted, filed, and reported. Change in level of treatment, including discharge, takes place by consulting a narrative "crosswalk," matching the patient's behaviors and needs to the appropriate types and intensities of service at any of ten levels of treatment.

For example (based directly on the information titled Crosswalk of Adult Admission Criteria, *ASAM PPC-2R*, p. 32) consider an adult who has been assessed as alcohol dependent and on dimension 4, readiness to change, shows little awareness and needs interventions available only at Level of Care III, which is clinically managed medium-intensity residential treatment. To be seen suitable at this level of care, the patient should also be showing mild to moderate severity in emotional, behavioral, or cognitive conditions and needing structure to focus on recovery. While in treatment at this level, the patient's conditions are clinically monitored to see whether a less or more intensive level of care is suitable. The monitoring is done, however, in a "holistic" way, tracking all dimensions of concern and all of the patient's behaviors. Since the *PPC* dimensions are problem-oriented, placement and changes take place according to the presence or absence of factors stated as "problems" or symptoms of problems. It keeps the monitoring staff alert for diminishing negative symptoms. As a medical-influenced model of planning, it makes a lot of sense. Again, there are no explicit measures of treatment response or recovery criteria, other than changes in the needed levels of care themselves, which might reflect how the patient is doing.

Patient Compliance

Since 1989, an increasing concern related to patient progress, namely patient compliance, has appeared. In their book, Daley and Zuckoff (1999) discuss improving treatment compliance; that is, how to keep the patient in treatment and working on the treatment plan. Patients exit treatment in many ways other than through successful discharge. They relapse and stop showing up; they miss appointments; they stop taking prescribed medications; they don't attend support meetings; they don't pay their bills; and so on. In the index of Daley and Zuckoff's book, under "recovery/monitoring," the reader is directed to a passage suggesting that counselors should monitor "the common issues faced by the client in recovery (e.g., cravings, desire to use, close calls, high-risk people, places, or events, motivation changes, boredom)" (p. 71). Lacking any suggestion on how to do this monitoring, we are left to conclude that it is done in one-on-one interviews and that clinical notes reflecting any concerns are then discussed with staff at meetings, shared with supervisors, or entered into *PPC* formats if changes are called for.

■

There are no quick and easy monitoring tools, it seems. No short tests, questionnaires, or surveys to determine treatment success or compliance. In some agencies, it comes down to whether or not the patient is still abstinent. Everything else hinges on that. In those agencies, monitoring tools are counselor "concerns" that try to predict or anticipate relapse, unless the counselor is regularly using Gorski's relapse-prevention inventories with patients.

Herein lies (just as in the situation for the delivery and recording of *treatment*) the *recovery* assessment dilemma. If a criterion for recovery like simple abstinence or reduced intake is used, the essence of recovery is overlooked, though measurement is easy. If the complexity and richness of the experience of recovery are the criteria (as suggested by counselor notes that go beyond the treatment plan to include news about the patient's inner well-being), then measurement is more difficult but more meaningful. This is a continuation and extension of the familiar debate between clinicians, psychometricians, and assessment professionals: the cost of using subjective reports as a measure of anything is the loss of reliability, possibly the loss of validity, and the inability to define the topic of interest with enough clarity to be scientific about it. The price of using solely objective data, such as compliance with treatment plans, records of arrests, court actions, and so on, is likely to be heavily negative. Record-keeping systems are usually set up to record only deficiencies, errors, and problems, rather than achievements or client feelings. Objective data do not capture what the experienced counselor can intuit about a client. Even when using the familiar "SOAP" method of recording patient problems and their resolution, in which the counselor records the patient's Subjective (symptom) statement, the counselor's Objective version of it, the Assessment of the situation, and the Plan needed to solve the problem, the data, like individual client records, remain difficult to combine across different patients.

Some attempts, discussed below, have made the subjective experiences of patients more objective and recordable in a systematic way.

Symptoms of Recovery

Hoffman and Estes (1986, 1987) created an inventory, called the Body/Behavioral Experiences (BBE) inventory, to measure the subjective reports of physical, emotional, and behavioral symptoms occurring in early recovery. Though Hoffman and Estes do not use the term "post-acute withdrawal" (Gorski 1986, 1989), their BBE inventory measures the extent of prolonged abstinence symptoms in recovering alcoholics. Hoffman and Estes were motivated to develop the BBE in part by a study by Massman (1979) on "normal recovery symptoms," or the common, recurring, and sometimes alarming symptoms affecting people during and after treatment. The BBE documents such physical experiences as increased desire for sugar (71 percent of sample), periods of increased energy (67 percent), food binges (62 percent), and weight fluctuations (55 percent). Behavioral experiences reported included fatigue during the day, feelings of sadness, irritability, jitteriness, and marked mood fluctuations in more than 70 percent of the sample. The mean length of abstinence when these symptoms were reported was twenty-seven weeks.

Several observations can be made about these results. First, these abstinence-based symptoms are viewed as measures of recovery in some sense. Second, these symptoms are considered normal for recovering people. Third, Massman believed there was no way to accelerate the recovery process to relieve these symptoms earlier. However, according to Blum, et al., recovery is "quickened" fairly easily with nutritional and neurochemical supplements. This raises a question: if such distresses as post-acute withdrawal symptoms signify recovery, then does lessening them through treatment mean that not as much recovery is occurring? For an analogy, consider a medical patient who has a tumor removed and one of the normal consequences is the minor pain (compared to tumor pain) of healing the wound. If there is pain, it may signify that healing is occurring and steps taken to reduce the pain may interfere with the healing process.

The pain of abstinence appears to be a necessary part of recovery. However, the post-acute withdrawal, the grief, and the pain of growth are part of *the cost of the disease, the price of recovery*, but not recovery itself. Most models of the recovery process are advisories on how to pay the price and descriptions of the tasks, turmoil, and hazards of getting well, rather than discussions of what is achieved or gained by this process.

Well, then, what is achieved? *In recovery, a person gets better and better at being Self, better at enjoying life, and better at knowing how to do the right thing while staying sober.* This does not happen quickly. Indeed, it does not happen until the second of two stages of recovery, described in the next chapter. However, even when it does happen, how do we know?

From this point on in this book, the goal is to find a way to identify and record the signals, signs, and symptoms of recovery so we can say, "Yes, this is what we mean by recovery. Look at this; here it is."

—*//*—

3

THE PUSH AND PULL
OF RECOVERY

Long-term recovery brings more than continued abstinence; at some point during recovery, many people gain an entirely new outlook on life. The extent of that transformation is evident in the range of answers I receive from recovering alcoholics to the following question: "Suppose you discovered that you have another disease, in addition to your alcoholism, but this other disease is not treatable, and you have only six months to live. Would you resume drinking?" Those in early recovery usually respond in this way: "Well of course I would; the main reason I stopped was because I was in desperate trouble, but if I were going to die anyway, why not drink?" However, later in recovery, people generally answer: "Well, no, I wouldn't start drinking again; that would spoil the six months I had left. I'd really want to be fully sober, to enjoy life to the end."

The first type of response is given in what I call the Push phase of recovery, whereas the second type of response is typical during the Pull phase. People in the first, or Push, phase, are fueled by the basic motivation of avoiding the consequences of drinking or drugging. They are "pushed" through their recovery activities by memory of the past and by fear of failure, relapse, or consequences of noncompliance with a treatment plan or a sponsor's advice. People in the Push phase see sobriety mainly as a matter of compliance. Some people never progress beyond this phase; they relapse before reaching the second, or Pull, phase. These people may adopt this Push orientation for the duration of a long but unhappy recovery.

The Pull phase, on the other hand, is marked by an enlarged outlook on the future. People in this phase of recovery are "pulled" into experiences and behaviors in pursuit of new goals. Now, recovery is more value-based than fear-based. People in the Pull phase can answer questions such as, "Who are your heroes? Has anyone, living or dead, real or fictional, led the kind of life you admire?" While those in the Push phase rarely have heroes, people in the Pull phase almost always do, and often have several. The difference seems to be whether a person can identify and endorse, even vicariously through a hero, a set of values.

Figures 1, 2, and 3 represent the main distinctions between the Push and Pull phases. The Push and Pull ideas are presented in figures 1 and 2 respectively, then are combined in figure 3. In figure 1, "degree of wellness" is measured over time, beginning with the onset of addiction. The left side of the figure, representing the period of time before treatment (Tx), depicts the downhill loss of overall wellness. At point P1, the person "hits bottom," meaning it doesn't get any worse than this in some sense. Treatment or some other intervention results in another point, P2, marking the uphill return to wellness. In a Push model of recovery (such as Gorski's 1986), all events in the recovery progression, depicted in the right-hand side of figure 1, refer to one of these two points, P1 or P2. That is, all events are related to the person's state of well-being at P1 or P2.

This notion is represented by the "eye" in figure 1, the client's literal point of view on recovery, looking back at the events leading to P1 or the events happening since P2.

FIGURE 1

The Push Model

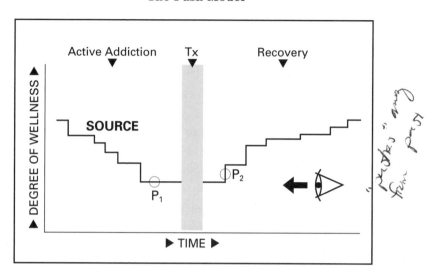

FIGURE 2

The Pull Model

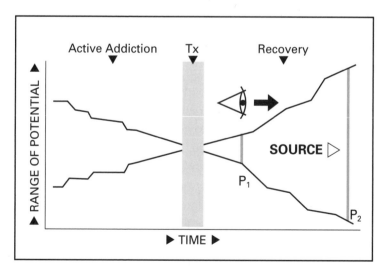

Phrases such as "when I hit bottom" or "when I did Step 1" reveal the person's orientation. However, the orientation goes even further psychologically. In the Push model, the basic motivation for sobriety and recovery lies in the past; the person is "pushed" by the fear of how it was, more than pulled by the potential of a better future. He or she is focused on recovery tasks, such as getting a sponsor, establishing regular eating habits, or discussing feelings, *because if these tasks aren't done, a relapse to point 1 or 2 levels of wellness is likely.* This model of recovery resembles a crisis intervention process, in which the person is being restored to a level of wellness that existed before the crisis but does not progress beyond that level. This person recovers "back to" a previous state.

Figure 2 contrasts certain aspects of a Push model with a Pull model. In Pull models (such as Maslow's works), something called "potential" or "wholeness" is the yardstick of measurement. In figure 2, this measurement is called "range of potential" rather than "wellness." Over time during active addiction, this range of potential becomes increasingly constricted, funneling the person into a point of debilitation. Most Pull models derive not from the study of chemical dependency but from general consideration of factors that limit the human potential. Alcoholism and other addictions certainly do this, but the Pull model owes more to the human potential movement than to the addictionology field. In figure 2, following treatment or therapy (Tx), the range of potential begins expanding from a point (P1) representing minimal capacity or motivation through and beyond another point (P2) at which the person's potentials reach his or her highest point to date. In a Pull conceptualization, people not only recover something that was lost but also develop new capacities. They develop new goals and values, trusting the unknown future more than the historic past. They are "pulled" in recovery by a set of values, people, ideas, or promises. Pull models, for these reasons, are more spiritually oriented than push models. The "eye" in figure 2 looks to the right, to the future, toward the east and the rising sun.

Both figures 1 and 2 include locations called Source, which refers to the origin of values and ideals that anchor the person's awareness, motivation, and trust. In figure 1, the Source comes from the person's past, before the onset of decline, part of the pre-addiction era. The values and ideals may derive from the person's family of origin. These values often present themselves during addiction and survive into the Push phase. Old rules such as "blood is thicker than water," "no sense in crying over spilled milk," or "you can't make a silk purse out of a sow's ear" characterize the person's thinking in the Push phase. In figure 2, however, the Source is out front, ahead, part of the recovery era. The values come from the principles the person is *following*, and the Source may be called the person's True Self, Conscience, or Higher Power. In any case (Push or Pull), the Source is at first ill defined but powerful.

The Two-Phase, Push-Pull Model

This chapter began with a discussion of Push and Pull as different *phases* of recovery rather than disparate alternatives. Figure 3 shows how these two phases are components of one model.

Figure 3 represents some of the basic theoretical stances of this book. The "yardstick" used to measure both the active and recovery phases of addiction appears on the left as "Actualizing Potential" (as described in Maslow's theory). During the active addiction phase, addicts experience a steady downward progression or lose actualizing potential. Self-esteem erodes; the person also loses the ability to get love and

FIGURE 3

Combination of the Push and Pull Models of Recovery

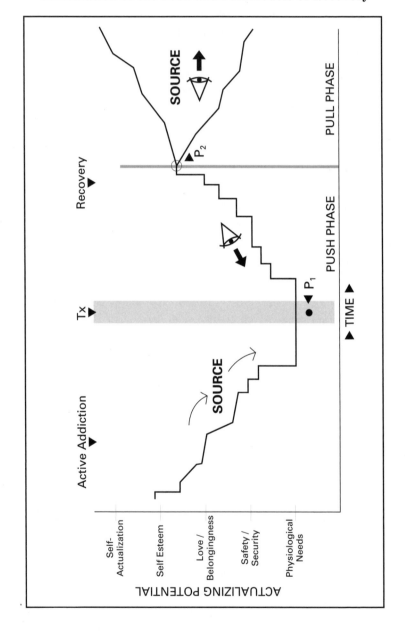

belongingness needs met, loses safety and security, and finally jeopardizes his or her physical wellness.

At P1 (treatment or any event that arrests active addiction) the Push phase of recovery begins. It corresponds to what will later be called "deficiency motivation," in which the person is (rightly) motivated by survival needs; at this point, higher needs go unmet. The "eye" of the client's perspective on recovery is directed toward P1, the onset of the Push phase.

The Pull phase begins at P2, after basic safety and security needs are met. At this point, the person is somewhere between meeting needs for love and belongingness and self-esteem. At P2 the basic process of recovery changes to a process best described as self-actualization. The person's Source of values shifts in the actualization process from something in the past to something in the present and future. The transition from the Push phase to the Pull phase may be sudden and dramatic. Some event such as the completion of a grief cycle may propel the person to P2. More often, however, it is a gradual shift. In the Push phase, the basic life-sustaining needs are being met, but needs relating to the enjoyment of that life are still unsatisfied.

Implications

Although treatment planning needs to address both phases of recovery, it's important to remember that the essence of recovery begins with the Pull phase, when life becomes enjoyable in a way not realized in the Push phase.[1]

This shift is often more evident in long-term outpatient settings than in an inpatient environment, because of the length of time required for a person to adjust to new ways of thinking and behaving. This two-phase model can also illuminate the belief that a Twelve Step program ultimately works the same way for all people, regardless of the disorder from which they suffer. Cermak (1986), for example, believes that after codependency is identified and the accompanying denial is broken, the recovery *process* from codependency is essentially the same as for chemical dependency, with the same eventual outcomes; namely, higher levels of self-actualization. In other words, the particular dependency in question— chemical dependency, codependency, gambling, overeating, sex, or any other—is first arrested in a Push phase that stresses the uniqueness of the disorder, along with attention to the negative markers of recovery. The Pull phase of recovery, which is essentially the same for all disorders, emphasizes the positive markers of recovery and the discovery and acceptance of Self.

Growing theoretical and empirical literature distinguish among different types of alcoholism, such as Cloninger's Type 1 and Type 2 alcoholisms. Such developments in the study of addictions may call for new treatment approaches to address the different profiles of these types. For instance, Type 1 shows hypervigilance without sensation seeking, while Type 2 shows the reverse. These differences may require somewhat different treatment models and reveal differences in how the types respond in the Push phase of recovery. However, the model here suggests that the Pull phase, once begun, will be essentially the same for all participants.[2]

—*//*—

4

THE ADMIT, ASK, ACT CYCLE

Many texts on counseling and interpersonal communications reveal a simple formula of how people change their feelings and behaviors. The formula goes like this: the person who is the "client" is encouraged (by the one who isn't) to do three things sequentially: *acknowledge* something is wrong or troublesome, explore or *ask* about helping resources or circumstances, and take *action* to resolve the problem. This is the basic approach underlying several kinds of cognitive-behavioral therapies, from Reality Therapy (Wubbolding 1988) to Morita Therapy (Reynolds 1984a, 1984b) to more recent models of solution-focused brief therapy (Berg and Miller 2000). This sequence of *admit, ask,* and *act* is a very natural process; children do it without much prompting. "Mom, I cut my toe," acknowledges the problem, which is followed by an inquiry for assistance, "Are there any bandages around here?" Action is taken by applying the offered bandage.

Often counselors are baffled when clients display reluctance to do any or all of these rather simple things. There are those people who, when in pain, simply can't, won't, don't *admit* it ("No, I'm fine; things are just fine"). There are those who can acknowledge or admit that something is wrong but don't *ask* about any solutions or help ("I always have had problems here; it's just the way things are. Can't change my personality"). And there are those who can admit and ask, but don't *act* on any idea or corrective measure ("Yes, I understand that this needs to be done, but I don't want to do it just yet").

When people willingly admit, ask, and act, they seem to be open, amenable to change, and energetic. "This doesn't feel right," a person admits. "I wonder what Bill might think about it," he asks, then acts by calling him right away.

The sequence of events is usually slower and richer than in this example, and it may take a great deal of effort to replace old, entrenched patterns of feeling, thought, and behavior. But the new pattern is acquired in some successful therapies and, most important, is inherent in the Twelve Steps of Alcoholics Anonymous. This sequence of Admit, Ask, Act, which I call the AAA cycle, can be found in the content and sequencing of AA's Twelve Steps (page 33).

Figure 4 illustrates the AAA Cycle of Change. Each Step is labeled as an Admit, Ask, or Act Step, according to the conceptualization above. Further, the boldface words indicate the kind of activity the Step involves. (Please note that this presentation of the Steps is not endorsed by Alcoholics Anonymous and should not be construed as an attempt to improve upon the Twelve Steps.)

In figure 4, note that Steps 1, 5, and 10 contain the word *admit*. Clearly the idea of these Steps is to acknowledge something. In Step 1, a person admits to being alcoholic and having an unmanageable life; in Step 5 the admission is to the exact nature of "wrongs"; and finally in Step 10, one admits to anything that seems wrong.

Fortunately "Ask" Steps follow each Admit Step. Step 2 suggests seeking help; Steps 6 and 7 suggest becoming willing and then asking for removal of character defects; Step 11 suggests asking for knowledge and power. Following each of the Ask Steps are Action Steps (3, 4, 8, 9, and 12). In these

The Twelve Steps of Alcoholics Anonymous*

1. We admitted we were powerless over alcohol—that our lives had become unmanageable.

2. Came to believe that a Power greater than ourselves could restore us to sanity.

3. Made a decision to turn our will and our lives over to the care of God *as we understood Him.*

4. Made a searching and fearless moral inventory of ourselves.

5. Admitted to God, to ourselves, and to another human being the exact nature of our wrongs.

6. Were entirely ready to have God remove all these defects of character.

7. Humbly asked Him to remove our shortcomings.

8. Made a list of all persons we had harmed, and became willing to make amends to them all.

9. Made direct amends to such people wherever possible, except when to do so would injure them or others.

10. Continued to take personal inventory and when we were wrong promptly admitted it.

11. Sought through prayer and meditation to improve our conscious contact with God *as we understood Him,* praying only for knowledge of His will for us and the power to carry that out.

12. Having had a spiritual awakening as the result of these steps, we tried to carry this message to alcoholics, and to practice these principles in all our affairs.

---

* The Twelve Steps of AA are taken from *Alcoholics Anonymous*, 3d ed., published by AA World Services, Inc., New York, N.Y., 59–60.

FIGURE 4

The AAA Cycle of Change
and the Twelve Steps of Alcoholics Anonymous

CYCLE ONE	*Admit*	1. We **admitted** we were powerless over alcohol—that our lives had become unmanageable.
	Ask	2. **Came to believe** that a Power greater than ourselves could restore us to sanity.
	Act	3. **Made a decision** to turn our will and our lives over to the care of God *as we understood Him.*
	Act	4. **Made a searching and fearless moral inventory** of ourselves.
CYCLE TWO	*Admit*	5. **Admitted** to God, to ourselves, and to another human being the exact nature of our wrongs.
	Ask	6. **Were entirely ready** to have God remove all these defects of character.
	Ask	7. Humbly **asked** Him to remove our shortcomings.
	Act	8. **Made a list** of all persons we had harmed, and became willing to make amends to them all.
	Act	9. **Made direct amends** to such people wherever possible, except when to do so would injure them or others.
CYCLE THREE	*Admit*	10. Continued to take personal inventory and when we were wrong promptly **admitted** it.
	Ask	11. **Sought** through prayer and meditation to improve our conscious contact with God *as we understood Him,* **praying** only **for** knowledge of His will for us and the power to carry that out.
	Act	12. Having had a spiritual awakening as the result of these steps, we tried to **carry this message** to alcoholics, and to **practice these principles** in all our affairs.

ADMIT *Process:* Acknowledging something is/was wrong; disclosing
ASK *Process:* Seeking assistance; turning to Sources other than self
ACT *Process:* Taking action on the basis of above; doing something

Steps, a person must make a decision, an inventory, a list, make amends, and practice principles and carry a message.

The Twelve Steps contain three cycles of the AAA process. The first cycle includes Steps 1 through 4, the next cycle includes Steps 5 through 9, and finally, the third cycle consists of the "growth-maintaining" Steps 10, 11, and 12.

The Steps, then, are arranged in an order that corresponds with a method some therapists have independently found to effectively facilitate change in people:

- first, getting in touch with feelings and attitudes, learning how to acknowledge them, especially by *naming* them;
- second, learning how to ask for assistance when needed, how to explore doubt, how to trust more;
- and finally, learning how to take prompt action, stop procrastinating and worrying, and be effective.

All of these facilitating features are built into the Twelve Steps and their sequencing. In short, the Twelve Steps teach people how to ask, admit, and act (AAA).

Alcoholics, addicts, and their families have little experience with the elements of the AAA process. Unbalanced family systems don't allow members to acknowledge what is really going on, name the problem as alcoholism, ask questions about it, trust that there is a different way, and act on the basis of suggestions from outside the system. Chemical dependency counselors are familiar with clients who come into treatment with little if any preparedness to admit to events, ask for help, or act on the basis of new information or ideas. Indeed, individuals may present the very opposite characteristics in the form of what I call the DIP (denial, insisting, passivity) process.

The Opposite of AAA is DIP

Here are the elements of the AAA process and their opposites:

Element	Opposite
Admission	Denial
Asking	Insisting
Action	Passivity

The DIP process describes relapse. People in danger of relapse are in *denial, insisting* on their own way, and showing *passivity* about most things. For example, a client named Harry comes to treatment with this outlook: "I don't have any feelings one way or the other on my family's participation" (denial); "well maybe I do have a problem, but I'll deal with it my way" (insisting); and, "right now I don't feel like going to a meeting; maybe in a few weeks" (passivity).

Variations on this basic DIP process are familiar to counselors: Gorski (1989) offers a relapse model in which this process occurs repeatedly. In his analysis, there is a relapse-prone "style" to which he gives the acronym ESCAPE: the person Evades or denies the stuck point, experiences Stress, shows Compulsive behavior, Avoids others, acquires new Problems, and then Evades these new problems, which sets the cycle in motion all over again. Gorski's six-stage "style" parallels the DIP process. The Evade stage corresponds to Denial; the Compulsive behavior corresponds to Insistence; and Avoiding corresponds to being Passive. Yet the DIP process, and its opposite in the AAA process, is simpler than the ESCAPE model (and its opposite, the RADAR model). Further, the DIP and AAA cycles may lend themselves to easier observation and measurement.

Treatment begins to make inroads by facilitating the weakening of the first element in the DIP process: denial. The

Twelve Steps continue working against the DIP elements by providing the exact antidote (AAA cycles) for the DIP process. This is why it's critical to work the Twelve Steps in order.

Applications

Many difficulties that arise during the recovery process, especially during the Push phase, are predicted by the AAA and DIP processes. Consider, for example, Carole, a woman who is fairly bright, intellectual, "self-sufficient in an insufficient way," who has difficulty asking for help but who has broken through her basic denial about being an alcoholic. Carole has the most difficulty on the ask Steps (2, 6, 7, and 11). She finds Steps 1, 5, and 10 easy enough to do (she doesn't have a problem with the admission Steps since her denial is broken), and she says Steps 4, 8, 9, and 12 feel "okay" when she thinks about them or begins working them. But on the ask Steps, which she sees as the "God Steps," she has turmoil. Perhaps Carole's turmoil is not so much that the asking Steps involve a Higher Power but that she has difficulty turning to resources other than herself, asking for something, and trusting she'll get what she needs.

On the other hand, consider Ron, who is stuck on the action Steps. Ron somehow can't sit down and write his inventory (Step 4). He easily becomes lost in thought. On Steps 8 and 9, he has no list and hasn't made any amends, saying, "I make amends by staying sober." Ron probably won't make direct amends until it becomes imperative. He believes that Step 12 and the principles of the program are easy to practice and "carrying the message" is rather effortless. He naively believes that practicing the principles means only having good thoughts, feelings, and *intentions*. He is passive. William James, whose influence extended into the formation of the Twelve Steps (Kurtz 1979) as well as into modern psychotherapy, characterizes this situation: "No matter how full a reservoir of maxims one may possess, and no matter how good one's sentiments may be, if one has not taken advantage of every concrete opportunity to act, one's character may remain entirely unaffected for the better." (James 1961, 14).

The various combinations of the AAA and DIP elements change a person over the course of recovery. Patients' turmoil is not necessarily a good or bad index of how they are practicing the Twelve Steps or following their conscience. Most people experience serenity only *after* experiencing long battles, rather than avoiding them. For some, turmoil is health; for others, turmoil kills. True recovery involves the discovery and separation of necessary versus unnecessary turmoil, appropriateness of pain, true costs versus the unnecessary expenses, with willingness and honesty versus mastery and endurance. Perhaps some of the unnecessary turmoil and confusion can be unraveled by looking carefully at something I call the "AAA Profile."

The AAA Profile

Counselors could gain a valuable head start on identifying patients' potential strengths and weaknesses in working the Twelve Steps by knowing patients' general history or attitudes regarding the AAA elements. Suppose we had some advance information about clients' tendency to be passive, coupled with information about their strengths in the elements of admitting and asking. This information, when shared with clients during an introduction to the Twelve Steps, might promote fruitful discussion on the challenges and opportunities for them personally.

A thirteen-item questionnaire, the AAA Profile taps into a person's general orientation on each of the three elements in the AAA cycle. The profile, found in appendix A, asks clients simply to read thirteen statements and indicate how each one applies to them. The statements are simple declaratives, such as "I do not like keeping secrets." Each element of the AAA cycle is probed four times. For example, the following four statements explore clients' belief or attitude about their ability to admit or acknowledge things:

- I admit when I am wrong.
- I do not like keeping secrets.
- I know when I'm not happy, but I don't talk about it.
- It takes a lot of evidence before I see something about myself I hadn't seen before.

The first and second statements are admissions in the active, or positive sense, while the second and third statements are negative (denial). The first statement correlates to Step 10; the second to Step 5; the third to general denial; and finally the last statement relates to Step 1. The relevant Steps are all Admit Steps.

Four different statements explore the person's asking abilities. Another four statements explore the person's orientation to action. The profile takes about five minutes to complete. The profile score indicates which of the three elements —Admit, Ask, or Act—is the most endorsed ("strongest") and which is the least endorsed ("weakest") characteristic of the client.

People with a weak Admit index, compared with a strong Ask index, may be able to ask for help more easily and do well on Steps 2, 6, 7, or 11; however, they may not understand what the help is supposed to be *for*. They are vague about the nature of their problems because they are weak in acknowledging or naming them. Similarly, people with a strong Act index but weaker Admit or Ask indexes may be "shoot first, figure it out later" sort of people, doing things impulsively. Such people may jump into making amends in Step 9 before doing any of the earlier Steps.

The profile is intended to be used "ideographically," with a single client at a time for purposes of self-comparison or as a discussion about successes or difficulties in approaching the Twelve Steps. The profile should not be used to categorize, screen, limit, or otherwise compromise the client's access to treatment. It is intended to be used when the client expresses confusion about difficulties working a particular Step or as a process-group activity. The AAA Profile can also be beneficial in small-group discussions about the Twelve Steps. Counselors using either motivational counseling or solution-focused models should be able to incorporate the AAA process and the profile into their practice with ease to assess readiness for and inducing expectations into the recovery process.

A fourth element that could be added to the AAA cycle is acceptance. Acceptance refers to "letting go" of outcomes once one's best effort has been given. It differs from Admitting because acceptance brings a wait-and-see curiosity rather than requests for answers or help. Sometimes acceptance is quickly followed by a new admission, a new release, a new cycle. In this way, acceptance may be an *outcome* of the AAA cycle, rather than part of the process. The acceptance that hopefully follows Step 4, allows, in a sense, the admissions in Step 5; the acceptance of outcomes of making amends in Step 9 may signal readiness for Step 10. Acceptance marks the end of the grief cycle as well as the completion of any cycle of change in which the action component, triggered by courage, is balanced by the need to stand powerless and accepting when our best efforts fail. The Serenity Prayer of Alcoholics Anonymous asks for the wisdom to know the difference between what can be changed and what cannot; hence the need for acceptance in partnership with action. This pattern of AAA, including acceptance, relates directly to the process of grief resolution, discussed in chapter 6. The element of acceptance is not put into the AAA sequence as a fourth element because it is not as apparent in the Twelve Steps as the other elements are. Acceptance may be considered not so much a part of the AAA process as the *result* of that process.

No one knows exactly how the Twelve Steps of Alcoholics Anonymous really work. What I offer here is one of many possible analyses of that recovery program. The reader is encouraged to consider others (for example, Kurtz 1979; Berenson 1988; Rogers, et al. 1988). Step 12 of the AA program says that the result of practicing the Steps is a spiritual awakening, not an immunity to relapse. I present the discussion of the DIP process because sometimes counselors and recovering people focus only on fending off denial, insistence, and passivity. The opposite of the DIP process, the AAA process, is not emphasized as often in professional counseling as it is in Twelve Step recovery. Counselors do not often observe that the AAA process may lead to a spiritual awakening. I am making the observation here because the argument of this book is that long-term recovery consists of being pulled by something, rather than being pushed by the fear of relapse. The prevention of relapse is not the same as the fostering of recovery. The fostering of recovery means the fostering of spiritual awakening. Eleven of the Twelve Steps are aimed in that direction, and counseling should be too. I think professional counselors would be more likely to take such an orientation if the notion of an "awakening" could be translated into terms more compatible with their training, more amenable to measurement, and less mysterious to them and their patients. The focus on the DIP elements is traditional and further supports the concept of "harm reduction," getting rid of the patients' liabilities, correcting their erroneous behavior, and showing them the danger signs. But the AAA process is not just an antidote for DIP elements that counteracts deficits and restores some semblance of normality. The AAA process is an engine that can power the recovery process beyond the bounds of normal wellness.

The AAA cycle is the central activity of such a process, but not the entire process. At some point, possibly at Step 2 for some, Step 6 for others, the content and meaning of the Twelve Steps start to matter just as much as the process of working them. The Steps talk about the restoration of sanity and the removal of defects and shortcomings by a God "as we understand Him." Step 11 talks of "conscious contact" with that God. What the recovering person learns is to practice the Steps, not to practice being God. A spiritual awakening is not *a* result; it is *the* result.

■

The next chapter will discuss self-actualization, which may be tantamount to a definition of spiritual awakening. Self-actualization for people in recovery comes about through the practice of the Twelve Steps and their underlying AAA cycles. For example, according to Maslow, self-actualizing people have a certain amount of spontaneity and self-esteem. They display those characteristics when admitting what is on their minds and in their hearts. They admit without unnecessary fear, hold few secrets, and are candid about their mistakes. Compare the wording of Steps 1, 5, and 10 in this regard.

Actualizing people are able to Ask for what they want and need, keeping in mind what they already have. They are able to "get out of themselves," trust others, and devote themselves to ideas outside of their own ego. In this regard, compare the wording of Steps 2, 7, and 11.

People who are self-actualizing know themselves and the extent of their influences (good and bad); they follow principles of self-conduct that reflect their own values. Compare Steps 4, 9, and 12 regarding the Acts of self-inventory, making amends, and practicing principles.

Adherents of the Twelve Steps know that the recovery process can result in lifelong changes in personality. *They know that the goal of sobriety is not to become "normal" but to transcend normality; self-actualizing people achieve the same goal.*

—//—

5

SELF-ACTUALIZATION

Understanding the process of recovery is of great importance, but so, too, is an analysis of the *result* of that process. The recovery process is essentially a process of actualization and the result is an actualizing Self. For people who are chemically dependent, the recovery process begins with abstinence and then proceeds into and through a hierarchy of stages that were suggested by the Push-Pull model in chapter 3. That model measures the recovering person's Actualization Potential. We now come to a discussion of what that is.

At times, we can better understand something by looking at the effects of its absence. The following quotation concerns a group of people who may be clients of counselors, therapists, and treatment institutions, but more often are not assisted by anyone, ever, with their problem:

> . . . They do not accept themselves; they have low self-esteem. They are not open to their environment and the experience of their organism and their senses; their relationships with reality are disturbed. They do not accept or respect others, and are disturbed in their interpersonal relationships. They are self-centered rather than problem-oriented (in the sense of devoting themselves to a problem or cause outside themselves). They are dependent, inhibited rather than spontaneous and wear a mask or facade rather than being real and genuine. Their creativity is suppressed, so that they are unable to utilize and develop their potentials. (Patterson 1985, 46)

These characteristics may sound familiar to chemical dependency counselors, because they are also common in alcoholics, addicts, and their families. But the author of this quote knows little of alcoholism and addictions. He is an expert in self-actualization psychotherapy and wrote about people who are not self-actualizing. Instead, they are caught up in *deficiency motivation*. They bear a remarkable resemblance to people stuck in the Push phase of recovery. Though alcoholism and other addictions are not *caused by* lack of self-actualization, addictions *guarantee interference with or a complete halt to self-actualization. Recovery means becoming self-actualizing.*

Here are four principles of this view of recovery as an actualizing process:

1. The diseases of alcoholism and other drug addictions make it impossible for people to progress into stable self-actualizing lives.

2. The goal of recovery is the same as the goal of life, namely actualization of the Self.

3. The process of recovery through Twelve Step programs is the process of self-actualization, beginning with abstinence and proceeding through deficiency motivation in the Push phase.

4. The characteristics of self-actualizing people are the same characteristics that recovering people aspire to in the Pull phase.

Abraham Maslow, a psychologist interested in the relationships between human motives, needs, and values, constructed a set of theories based on what he called the hierarchy of human motivations (Maslow 1954). Figure 5 shows the hierarchy. Human needs are arranged from basic needs for food, water, air, whatever maintains our normal physical health, at the bottom of the hierarchy (or pyramid) in the zone called "physiological needs." In an upward direction we find safety and security, love and belongingness, self-esteem, and finally self-expression. Maslow considered the first two levels basic, or lower-level, needs and said that until they were met, a person could not effectively get higher-order needs met. The first two levels are considered survival needs; the next three make survival worth it.

FIGURE 5

Maslow's Hierarchy of Needs / Motivation

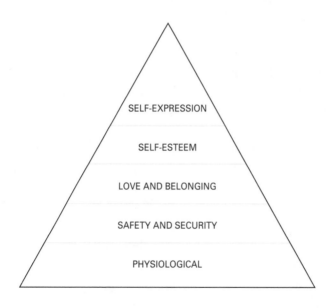

The needs (and the motivations geared to meeting them) in figure 5 are arranged in a vertical order and must be met *in that order*, or something goes wrong in the basic effort of that person to be fully human. The hierarchy of figure 5 suggests, for example, that a person who is getting his physiological needs and his safety and security needs met, but has not made any progress on his sense of being loved and belonging to something or some group, cannot progress in the area of self-esteem. Similarly, the time to work on love and belongingness is *after* making progress in the zone below it; namely, safety and security. Said simply, a person cannot profit much from reading books or attending sessions on intimacy and self-esteem if she has no place to live or feels emotionally unsafe.

Maslow and his followers like Patterson maintained that humans are intrinsically motivated or "pre-wired" to achieve satisfaction at all levels of the hierarchy and are capable of the highest level, self-expression. At this level, people are not stressed by physical or emotional needs but accept problems out of curiosity, a need to understand, or from a uniquely human attitude about life. Maslow argued that the people functioning at this level must do what they are doing to be at peace with themselves because the genuine and authentic Self demands, deserves, and thrives on expression. Thus, the musician plays, the writer writes, the hiker hikes, the mother provides. Note that this does not happen with any regularity unless the lower-level needs are satisfied or at least not consuming the person's time and attention. Maslow's extension of these ideas evolved into a whole new area of study in psychology, namely Transpersonal Psychology. Maslow authored the first paper in volume one of the journal *Transpersonal Psychology* in 1969. He died in 1970; the journal continues.

Patterson (1985), translating Maslow with a more contemporary vocabulary, summarizes what people are like when they are successfully self-actualizing:

> People have a single basic motivation, the preservation and enhancement of the self, or the drive toward self-actualization
> ... Among other characteristics of the self-actualizing person

is the ability to develop good interpersonal relationships. This involves acceptance and respect for others, understanding or empathy with others, and openness, genuineness, or honesty in interpersonal relationships. Self-actualizing persons accept themselves and their human nature with its fallibilities. They are secure and thus do not have to be defensive; they are not easily threatened. They are in close touch with their environment, being sensitive and aware of stimuli. Their locus of control is internal rather than external, so that they are autonomous, independent, and develop their own value systems. (pp. 45–46)

Table 2 details Patterson's and Maslow's descriptions. These characteristics are often considered the composite portrait of an ideal therapist, which supports the notion that a counselor must be operating under motivations higher on the Maslow hierarchy than the client. This means that the best therapist who can professionally assist a client with unmet needs in the self-esteem area is a self-actualizing therapist/ person whose counseling is part of an ongoing self-expression process and who possesses the characteristics in table 2.[1]

Patterson maintains that all people ultimately want these characteristics, but most people get stuck by environmental deprivations, emotional and nurturing deprivations, and by diseases at a level of striving or motivation below the upper levels on the hierarchy. Maslow (1971) distinguished two major types of motivational "clusters." One he called deficiency motivation, which is geared to *survival* and *self-preservation*. Deficiency motivation involves avoidance of hunger, thirst, discomfort, conflict with others, insecurity, failure, or abandonment. It is seen in the Push phase. It does not mean that recovery is not happening. On the contrary, recovery is proceeding but only with little joy and a lot of worry. The second type of motivation, which leads to self-actualization, is termed

TABLE 2

Characteristics of Self-Actualizing People

(based on narrative descriptions in Patterson 1985, 39–41)

Characteristic	Correlates with
1. Efficient perception of reality	Openness to environment
2. Acceptance of self and others	Honesty, genuineness, esteem
3. Spontaneity	Internal motivation
4. Problem-centeredness	Not ego-centered; mission oriented
5. Detachment	Need for privacy; non-isolating in solitude
6. Autonomy	Internal locus of control
7. Freshness of appreciation	Sense of wonder and awe; peak experiences
8. Empathy	Compassion for humanity and specific people
9. Deep interpersonal relations	Small circle of close friends
10. Democratic character	Non-prejudicial; humility
11. Ethical	Sense of fairness, justice
12. Sense of humor	Unhostile laughter and amusement
13. Creativeness	Fresh outlook; divergent thinking

being motivation. Deficiency and being motivation each have their own form of thinking or cognition: Deficiency cognition, associated with deficiency motivation, is self-centered, pragmatic, either-or, humorless, fear-based, and demands decisions and actions leading to survival. It is characteristic of people described in the first quotation from Patterson on nonactualizing people and is very similar to what life is like for a person *stuck* in the Push phase of recovery. Being cognition, associated with being motivation, is a conscious state of thoughtful acceptance. It is nonjudgmental, active, based on wonder, curious, responsible, and allows most of the characteristics in table 2 to appear. It is what starts happening in the Pull phase of recovery.

Nothing in Maslow's presentation of the hierarchy of needs or in the discussion here implies that failure to reach these higher needs *causes* alcoholism or addiction. The disease concept of alcoholism locates addictions at the very foundation of the pyramid, as a threat to the physiological well-being of the person whose genetic vulnerability is itself located at that level. Recovery has to be from the bottom up, starting with the physiological stabilization of the abstinent person. We have to ensure safety and security while the person's denial systems are weakened.[2] As diseases, alcoholism and other drug addictions shake the whole hierarchy. They do not disappear with momentary increases in self-esteem or belongingness, or with fitful attempts at self-expression (writing poetry in the back of the room while another patient is sharing his or her First Step). No lasting improvement in those areas occurs until drinking and drugging stops. These illnesses guarantee a fight for survival in their primary victims and those around them. This struggle for survival, both in the active disease *and in early recovery*, produces a fear-based motivation similar to deficiency-motivation. In later recovery, however, the motivation changes to something like being motivation. Some models of recovery are Push models, capitalizing on fear-based deficiency cognition and deficiency motivation. The recovery model in this book and some others are about the shift from survival to enjoyment of life. In my opinion, that is what the Twelve Steps, the Promises, and the legacies of Alcoholics Anonymous are about: *the responsible enjoyment of life.* Self-actualization, a value-based rather than fear-based process, replaces the Push phase of early recovery and begins the Pull phase of ongoing, continuous recovery.

So if the Push phase is a necessary part of recovery, the part in which the person, now abstinent, is still locked into the past and has not entered into the dynamics of the Pull of self-actualization, how do we facilitate that entrance and not just content ourselves, as counselors, with having saved another person from the agonies of continued alcohol and other drug use? How do we detect or create readiness for the Pull phase? What central events can change the recovery light from yellow to green? What has to happen in the Push phase, above and beyond stabilization and the weakening of denial and the introduction of a recovery program, to usher in the Pull phase? What needs to happen at P2 in figure 3?

One of the key events in fashioning the shift from Push to Pull, deficiency to being motivation, is the grief syndrome, the painful contact with past losses, the proto-spiritual awakening to a life ahead. For this reason, grief is the topic of the next chapter. Maslow's conception of belonging needs and of self-esteem are considered in the chapter after that.

—//—

6

GRIEF

Addiction means loss. In active addiction, losses include values, money, friendship, hope, and integrity. When the addiction is arrested by treatment and abstinence, the addict experiences a crushing loss of the drug itself—alcohol, cocaine, nicotine, or pot. All the molecular treats that had been so welcomed and so important in the addict's life are gone.

A grief syndrome accompanies the loss of important things. We usually associate grief with the loss of a loved one. But that is called bereavement, which the American Psychiatric Association classifies as an adjustment disorder. It is not a mental illness. On the contrary, it shows the person's mental state is normal, because bereavement is seen as a "normal" part of life. Bereavement is a subclassification of grief, which is more widespread.

According to Kübler-Ross (1969), we experience grief when we lose anything of importance, and grief is not limited to bereavement over a lost loved one. In recovery, the grief syndrome begins the moment patients contemplate the loss of their drug of addiction, as well as the loss of whatever routines and people supported that addiction. Recovery means change. Initially, in the Push phase, change means loss.

Grief's role as an element in the recovery process has been largely overlooked. With the notable exception of Middleton-Moz and Dwinell's *After the Tears* (1986) and pamphlets by

Kellerman (1992) and McDonald (1996), few training materials for chemical dependency counselors discuss grief counseling. Instead, counselors have been trained to recognize and treat something called post-acute withdrawal (PAW), a syndrome affecting recovering people in the first three to six months of abstinence (see Gorski 1989). The PAW syndrome includes extensive grief, signaling the arrival of defenses against a new kind of pain—the sobering pain of losses that cannot be dulled with usual defenses (drug use); this pain calls for a different kind of management. (Of course, there is a lingering physio-logical and psychological imbalance that deserves the term post-acute withdrawal. Nonetheless, the grief syndrome may be hidden or ignored in PAW and should not be.)

In recovering people, grief can lead either to extended chronic grief, which locks people in the Push phase until they relapse, or to an awakening which can propel them into the Pull phase. This section is intended to point out opportunities to document, evaluate, and promote the recovery process, rather than sounding alarms about all that can go wrong as people respond or don't respond to treatment and recovery programs.

Identifying grief as a syndrome calls attention to the variety of signs, pathology, and symptoms that comprise it, whether the symptoms occur simultaneously or sequentially. A syndrome is a collection of diverse signs and symptoms that, when considered singly, do not carry the full meaning or potential significance of the whole. In other words, one plus one plus one equals seven. For example, if you were to see your physician about a headache, the physician would proba-bly inquire about other symptoms you might be experiencing, rather than immediately prescribing a pain reliever and send-ing you on your way. If you were to tell the physician that you also were feeling very stiff and sore in your neck, the physi-cian might ask about when that pain overlapped with the head pain. At this point, both symptoms could have numerous causes, including stress. Suppose you next inform the medical doctor that you also have, periodically, a strong aversion to bright lights. The physician might then order a series of tests and conduct a special examination, because the three symptoms might all be caused by meningitis, a disease more serious than any of the three individual symptoms indicate.

So it is with grief. The individual behaviors of denial, anger, "pink-cloud" optimism, and depression are all part of the syndrome. Their combined meaning is more significant than that of any of the individual behaviors. When seen as part of grief, depression may be treated in a way very different from the treatment of endogenous clinical depression. Indeed, in the former case, the best "treatment" may be none at all. Similarly, when anger is part of a grief syndrome, it takes on different features and deserves a different kind of attention than when it is a reactive response to a frustrating roadblock.

If you, like myself, know many people with three or more years of sobriety, it is almost certain that every one of them has completed a grief syndrome. Grief, as we will see, is one of the "tests" of a person's recovery. Grief inevitably happens to all recovering people who are not psychopaths,[1] and it is never pleasant. It's impossible to make grief a comfortable experience. There are, however, ways to make it explicit and to incorporate it into a person's recovery, if we know how to recognize it and especially know what not to try to do. The people who get through it are the ones who enter the Pull phase, which time alone cannot give and which a counselor alone must not attempt to control.

Next, the elements of the grief syndrome will be described first as they occur in the more familiar form of the bereavement process and then as they relate to the realm of addiction and recovery. The elements are the same in each case, and the sequence may be the same, but the "volume" or intensity of each may differ, as well as the duration.[2]

The Grief of Sarah

Sarah and George have enjoyed a strong marriage for forty years. Now their children are grown and have moved away, and George is about to retire from his career as a chemist in a large corporation. He has scheduled a physical examination required for the insurance program that will cover him in his retirement years. Sarah accompanies him to the physician's office; both of them think his exam will be brief and they plan to spend the remainder of the day buying a motor home in which they plan to travel for a few years. They are excited about this, just as they have been excited about many of the events they have planned together during the decades of their marriage.

Sarah waits in the reception area while George is in with the doctor, who has been their family physician for many years. After two hours, Sarah is growing restless and somewhat annoyed at how long the exam is taking. Then the doctor calls her in to an examining room, saying that he needs to talk with her. George is not there.

Shock

"Sarah," says the physician, "I need to tell you the results of my examination of George." The physician knows about the grief and bereavement process—he has done this many times. He knows the first stage of grief is sometimes shock and expects Sarah to respond accordingly. He carefully observes Sarah's reaction to the bad news he is about to deliver, because her response, the shock, should not last for more than a few minutes. He knows not to try to break the news and comfort her at the same time. He respects her and will respect her grief.

"During my examination of George I discovered a lump that concerned me, so I performed a quick biopsy. The results indicated cancer. I had another test performed, and it, too, was positive for cancer. Sarah, George has an advanced form of cancer that we cannot cure. George has about four months to live."

In the shock stage, Sarah is emotionally numb. She is not in denial, nor is she angry or depressed. She says things such as, "What? What did you say? What are you saying?" The doctor repeats the information as often as needed, as clearly as possible, until he sees that she has left the shock stage and entered the next phase, denial.

Denial

"Oh, there is some mistake!" says Sarah. "That can't be; George is healthy as a horse. What kinds of tests did you do? How dare you say something like that!" And she begins to cry. She is not crying because she thinks George is going to die: she is crying because she is so offended that the doctor could say such things, which she knows can't be so. She is upset because she was unprepared for anything like this and now faces the burden of understanding why this doctor is saying such things about George.

Denial is the first line of defense against the pain of loss. Sarah is not "deceiving" herself, covering up, avoiding the issue, or trying to "save face." She simply believes that this news cannot be correct, that a mistake of huge proportion has been made. She believes this for a good reason—the pain of the prospective loss of George is too enormous. Denial is one of several defenses against such pain, and Sarah will use more, as needed. In grief, people do not feel the pain of loss as long as these defenses are operating. Sarah is not addicted to any drug, so she has only the psychological defenses of denial, anger, and depression available. For active addicts and alcoholics, however, the pain-numbing effects of drugs often replaces the more usual defenses. That is why active addicts cannot complete a grief syndrome. Because they use drugs instead of the usual defenses of denial, anger, and depression, they cannot reach the final stage of grief—the acceptance of the pain. Addicts don't experience the grief associated with their addiction until they become abstinent and enter recovery. At this point, the grief syndrome appears and must be recognized.

Sarah will stay in the denial phase of grief until something quite explicit happens. She will eventually *acknowledge* that George is indeed going to die, after seeing the medical evidence, getting a second opinion, and maybe, especially, talking to George. "Sarah," he might say, "I knew I was sick with something. My appetite had changed, and I had to get up in the night a lot. I didn't want to worry you. I believe the doctor is right." Denial weakens or breaks when the person admits or acknowledges some evidence or circumstance. But the absence of denial does not mean the person is now defenseless against the pain of loss. In grief and bereavement, the next defense to appear is often anger.

Anger and Bargaining

Sarah is angry at George ("You idiot! Why couldn't you tell me about this? How often had I told you not to work around dangerous chemicals?"). She is angry at the doctor ("The fool! Why didn't he spot this two years ago, when it might have been treatable?"). She is angry at herself ("What kind of wife have I been if he couldn't confide in me? Why didn't I see these changes in him?"). She is angry and blaming but may not show her feelings outwardly, depending on how her family legacy has shaped her expression of anger. In some families, especially authoritarian and drug-affected families, the expression of anger is essentially forbidden. Sarah may internalize her feelings, becoming silent and remote.

Anger in the grief syndrome serves a purpose. It diminishes the experience of the pain that comes with the loss. As evidence that this is so, Sarah's anger may evaporate immediately if she has reason to believe that the loss may not happen after all, that is, if she has hope. Suppose she sees a magazine article on new "miracle cures" for cancer: a new clinic in Switzerland (she reads) promises a cure for exactly the kind of cancer afflicting George; all it takes is $70,000 and thirty days. She excitedly tells George about her "discovery." In her hope, she enters the bargaining stage of grief ("George, we can sell the house and go to Switzerland and get you cured and have a wonderful trip at the same time!"). Her anger has disappeared entirely. Eventually, however, hope may run out when the information about a cure proves to be false. Sarah may then use her last defense against the pain of loss— depression.

Depression

Depression is not a conscious choice, either within the grief syndrome or outside of it. None of these defenses is. Depression works to dull pain because it dulls nearly all experience, internal and external. It is kind of a "shotgun" defense —Sarah doesn't feel pain but also doesn't feel pleasure, joy, anger, curiosity, or serenity. She may spend hours in bed or feel listless. She shuts down. As she does so, the pain gathers volume and she feels some of it and cries *because it hurts.* It hurts physically, mentally, and spiritually.

At this point, people go in one of two directions: they either continue defending against the pain or they drop their defenses and experience the pain. This is a critical time, because if Sarah is not allowed or is unable to bear the pain, she may resort to any of the previously used defenses (denial, anger, bargaining) and enter into what can be termed extended or chronic grief, a life-debilitating situation often misdiagnosed (as bipolar disorder, a personality disorder, or post-traumatic stress, for example). Chemically dependent people are at high risk of relapse now. Many will display the "dry-drunk" or "white-knuckle" kind of existence familiar to their counselors and friends.

Acceptance

In order to reach the last stage of the grief syndrome, called acceptance, people need to do something very difficult for themselves, their friends, family, and counselors. They need to experience the pain of the loss. This means surrendering their defenses. That is very hard to do, especially for people who have regularly defended themselves against pain with drugs. But it must be done. Under the best circumstances, it can be done alone, but this creates a high risk of relapse or a return to chronic grief. Instead, friends and counselors can be ready to assist the person who is experiencing the grief by helping the person *not do it alone.* All the helper has to do is be there, watch, listen, and not interfere by offering comfort in the form of "talking them out of their pain." In other words, we help most by letting others cry when they feel grief.

During the acceptance stage, we must be careful in identifying what is being "accepted." It is not the loss itself that is accepted as "okay." In Sarah's case, she is not accepting George's death. Rather, she is accepting the *pain of* the loss, not the loss itself. Sarah may still feel, twenty years later, that it was a shame, a terrible thing, that George died at age sixty-five, but if she has experienced most of the related pain by crying and accepting, her life will not be scarred.

Right now, in some hospital somewhere, a young couple is contemplating the impending death of their child. Maybe leukemia is about to claim the life of their seven-year-old daughter. Hopefully, none of us, not one, would tell those parents that they will just have to accept the death of their child. That child's death is not acceptable. We'd commit serious social and spiritual error to say, "Oh, that happens; just accept it." Instead, we hope those parents come to terms with the *pain* of the loss, but not come to "terms" with the loss itself. They will forever wish that their child had not died, but they will have experienced and survived the pain of it. In that sense, and only that sense, will they have achieved "acceptance" of the pain.

Grief in Recovery

Applying these observations to people in recovery, imagine a person named Bill, age thirty-five, who has three months of abstinence in an outpatient treatment program. He has been writing out his First Step, describing his history of powerlessness over alcohol and marijuana and how his life had become unmanageable (unmanageable by himself, and hence identifying people who were managing things for him). Now we ask him to draw from his writings a list of important things he lost. These would be things he sees as truly lost, not just misplaced. Many may be things he feels are irreplaceable.

Suppose his loss list looks something like this:

- my marriage to Eileen;
- the job at the Northfield Foundry;
- the 1965 Mustang I was rebuilding;
- the scholarship I had, but never used, to attend North River College;
- custody of my son Jack;
- the respect of my son Jack;
- Jack himself;
- my self-respect;

- my dreams of having a cabin on the lake;
- all the pictures and albums that burned up in the apartment fire;
- my best friend, Tom, from high school;
- my grandfather, who died alone while I was on a binge in New Orleans;
- my sister, Karen, who hasn't talked to me in eight years.

Now we ask Bill whether he has ever grieved those losses. He says, "Sure, I cried in my beer over every one of them." Someone in Bill's group may point out that what Bill experienced was probably self-pity, the kind that mixes well into alcohol, and that if he were drunk, then he never felt any nontoxic pain over those losses. Bill may have felt pangs and sharp edges, and he may have felt sorrow, but the alcohol and the marijuana prevented him from experiencing the real pain of his losses. Although he can acknowledge the existence of those losses, he is far from having accepted their pain, because he hasn't *felt* the pain. He hasn't yet been in what we call grief. If he stays clean and sober, the grief will come. Either he can expect or prepare for it, or the grief can catch him on the couch on a Sunday afternoon, momentarily defenseless as tears well up and he is without a clue as to what is happening. His primary defense against pain has been alcohol or other drugs. In the early stage of recovery, he may turn to them now, especially if he treats these new discomforts in the DIP (denial, insistence, passivity) fashion.

Such losses don't happen only to thirty-five-year-old men with twenty years of addiction bringing on those losses. There are fourteen-year-old kids on the streets who have lost virtually everything of importance to them, whose grief-anger takes the form of outrage and violence, and whose grief-depression takes the form of suicide. Their defense against pain may not be as sophisticated as Bill's denial, yet they also experience denial, insistence, and passivity that characterizes addicted people. And these substitutes for the normal forms of grief are making them age so rapidly that they resemble eighty-year-old people stuck in chronic grief after a lifetime of loss. One defense they use effectively is keeping everything at an arm's length; they never let anything become too important to them. This strategy protects them, they think, from the pain of loss. This explains their indifference to or outright rejection of things that are usually considered important in life, such as education and family.

Turning back to Bill's story, we see that if Bill is not able to grieve his losses, he may remain in the Push phase—and his motivation for sobriety remains fear-based, since he can't make peace with or accept his past pain. What we hope is that he will reach a point, P2 in figure 3, at which his practice of the Twelve Steps and the Admit, Ask, Act cycles brings him into contact with the grief of those losses and that he works through this point without relapsing. For this to happen, we must prepare Bill for his experience of the pain of those losses, which were ignored or denied in his using days. Basically, the counselor will provide a "safety net" in which the defenseless griever can feel protected against external distractions (and "musts" and "shoulds") and also provide what Dwinell has called a "cognitive life raft" (Middleton-Moz and Dwinell 1986). This "raft" gives people the information they need to name their pain as grief rather than craziness, emotionality, or some other negative label.

The chart on page 65-66 summarizes the features of the grief process. Although the stages of grief are presented in the order identified by Kübler-Ross and others, the pattern that behaviors may occur varies from situation to situation.

Further, people may be experiencing grief for more than one loss, so they could be in the denial stage in one process, the anger stage in another, and the depression stage in yet another. Bill, in the above scenario, does not have to anticipate a separate grief syndrome for each of his losses. According to a phenomenon called *recruitment*, multiple and seemingly separate losses are *recruited* together into one knot of pain (see Middleton-Moz and Dwinell 1986). When this happens, people may feel as if they are "going crazy." They have mixed feelings of confusion, anxiety, frustration, weepiness, cravings, and all of the symptoms of post-acute withdrawal. What they need is some reassurance, if it is diagnostically true, that they are not crazy and terminally unique. They also need to be told that these things will not just "pass" easily on their own. Rather, they need help to see that they have lost some important things in their life, many of them connected to their addictions, and that it says something meaningful about them as people that they find it painful. This is part of the necessary suffering of recovery.

There is an answer in each person to the question "What is important to you?" The answer is often in what the person profoundly misses, once it is gone. If he or she is alcoholic, he or she will profoundly feel alcohol's absence. If it is love and honor, he or she will profoundly miss those too. If we try to prevent grief by talking people out of crying, encouraging them to keep their chemical painkillers handy, then we are not honoring their losses. Instead, we are prolonging the time in which they are unable to risk new adventures. The experience of pain in grief is necessary. The pain does not cause damage and instead signals healing.

The Grief Syndrome

Reactions to the Loss of Something Important
Based on Kübler-Ross (1969)

Grief is identifiable in three forms: acute, extended, and chronic. The signs and symptoms of each are as follows:

- *Acute grief:*
  Physical reactions/actions involving body stress every twenty to forty minutes, such as tightness in throat, loss of appetite, sighing and shortness of breath; sleeplessness; reports of emptiness, exhaustion.

- *Extended grief:*
  Feelings of guilt over failure to do something; feeling need to "do something" but lack of energy to do it; restlessness and aimlessness; exaggerated self-accusation or grandiosity; avoidance of others; blank staring for extended periods of time; emotional flatness.

- *Chronic grief:*
  Includes most of the features of extended grief, plus: tendency to become isolated as individual or family; high level of irritability; hostility toward friends and relatives; eroded self-esteem; jealousy and envy; resentment; seeming to be clinging and needy, alternating with rejection of help.

The resolution of grief occurs in stages. When these stages progress normally during acute or extended grief, they may be classified as an adjustment disorder.

continued on next page

In extended grief, which becomes chronic, the person keeps recycling through stages 2 through 5, not reaching stage 6. In order to reach stage 6, acceptance of the pain of the loss, the person must experience the pain. Stages 1 and 4 may not occur in all cases. The event or behavior, which ends that stage, is given in italics.

1. **Shock:**
   (emotionally numb; very brief)
   .... *clarity*

2. **Denial:**
   (blindness to and confusion about "facts")
   .... *acknowledgment*

3. **Anger:**
   (blaming, projecting; frustration; self-accusation)
   .... *hope leads to 4*
   .... *hopelessness leads to 5*

4. **Bargaining:**
   (gullibility, "pink cloud," pleading, controlling)
   .... *helplessness*

5. **Depression:**
   (shutting down, aimlessness, isolation)
   .... *abandoning defenses and feeling the pain*

6. **Acceptance** of the pain of the loss:
   (normalization; spiritual awakening in terms of feeling a relief from the burden of the pain; sadness over loss, but no lingering painfulness needing defenses against it)

The unnecessary suffering—namely, the lack of hope—doesn't have to happen. If grief is not anticipated, identified, and encouraged, and if the acceptance stage is not reached, the benefits of recovery in the Pull phase may not materialize. To enter into that phase, people need to believe that the grief will not keep returning. They need an expectation that life can and will be different, in a positive direction, and that they are not going to keep losing important things and people. They need to expect that they will, instead, acquire things that few of them have ever had. They need to understand what the man next to them at the latest Twelve Step meeting meant when he said, "Hi, my name is Bill, and I'm a grateful alcoholic." The things many people become grateful for are described in the next chapter, The Promises.

7

THE PROMISES

Near the end of many AA meetings, the following passage from *Alcoholics Anonymous* (1976) is read aloud. Sometimes the topic of the meeting is the passage itself, which is commonly called "the Promises."

> If we are painstaking about this phase of our development, we will be amazed before we are half way through. We are going to know a new freedom and a new happiness. We will not regret the past nor wish to shut the door on it. We will comprehend the word serenity and we will know peace. No matter how far down the scale we have gone, we will see how our experience can benefit others. That feeling of uselessness and self-pity will disappear. We will lose interest in selfish things and gain interest in our fellows. Self-seeking will slip away. Our whole attitude and outlook upon life will change. Fear of people and of economic insecurity will leave us. We will intuitively know how to handle situations which used to baffle us. We will suddenly realize that God is doing for us what we could not do for ourselves. (pp. 83–84)

The Promises are presented in table 3 with an interpretation of what each suggests. This allows a comparison between the Promises and the characteristics of self-actualizing people, page 50. Coming on the heels of the discussion of grief in the last chapter, we might now better appreciate the tremendous lure and power of the Promises for people emerging from the experiences of early recovery. These Promises not only offer hope to people experiencing grief and other stresses of the Push phase of recovery, but also can be used as the basis of evaluating the patient's status in the Push-Pull process. The Promises can be a series of benchmarks to measure whether abstinence is leading to increased self-actualization.

The Promises Checklist was developed to translate the Promises into an easy-to-use inventory to assess aspects of recovery. Using the Promises as a conceptual basis has the following seven theoretical and practical advantages:

1. People who are experts at recovery, namely those who are continuing AA members, endorse the Promises.

2. The Promises are stated in the form of *can*, *will*, or *discover* rather than *shoulds*, *oughts*, or *musts*.

3. The Promises overlap the concepts of self-actualization enough so that the basic idea of recovery as actualization is retained, but the checklist items come from the literature on recovery rather than the literature on actualization, making the underlying value system agreeable to people who are practicing a recovery program based on the same literature as the checklist.

4. Five of the Promises refer to the *absence* of negative feeling, while seven refer to the onset of revitalizing, positive feelings. There is a balance of recognition of a history of problematic negative markers (as in the Push process), and attention to new, positive markers and attitudes (as in the Pull process).

5. Since the Promises are presented in *Alcoholics Anonymous* and are imbedded in the Twelve Step program, patients are often familiar with them. This

TABLE 3

The Promises, adapted from *Alcoholics Anonymous*

Promise	Suggests
1. Freedom	freedom from worry, guilt, shame freedom to choose and act freedom from compulsive acts
2. Happiness	pleasure in self, others enjoyment of life
3. Absence of regret	no secrets, no regret no fear of blame no chronic grief
4. Serenity	peace of mind acceptance clear conscience
5. Benefits to others	experience not wasted interest in fellowship desire to help
6. Absence of self-pity	no feelings of uselessness no feelings of being a victim absence of false pride, martyrdom
7. Interest in others	curiosity and wonder about others empathy and care awareness of commonalities
8. Absence of selfishness	less self-preoccupation openness to others willingness
9. New attitudes	new outlook on life new values, beliefs honesty, optimism
10. Absence of fear of people	non-isolating new self-confidence, self-worth nondefensive humor
11. Absence of fear of economic insecurity	fewer money worries trust and patience in work spirituality
12. Intuitive abilities	new habits, new risks trust in sobriety less fretting and perfectionism
13. Higher Power realization	not alone, not-God

familiarity provides an easy transition to this recovery inventory.

6. Using a set of items based upon *an already endorsed and cherished set of criteria for recovery* should be advantageous over any laboriously derived set of standards from neutral observers' opinions.

7. Rather than trying to measure the emerging traits of potentially self-actualizing people, a better index might result from assessing the person's experience of the benefits of sobriety and using this sobriety for an enhanced life. The Promises refer to specific *experiences* of recovering people. Measuring experiences rather than traits avoids the issue of personality. Recovery is indeed the evolution of new characteristics in personality, but to measure personality per se is to fall into the historical debate about alcoholic or addictive personalities rather than to focus on what shapes the changes in a recovering person's life. This book argues that it is experience—the working of the Twelve Steps and their AAA cycles—that shapes changes. The Promises are an index of the outcomes of that work and are the symptoms of recovery.

Finally, there is an important interplay between the expectations embodied in any "testing materials" and the expectations of the test taker. The inventory that tests for the attainment of or progress toward a *goal* is always preferable over one that simply tests for the existence of some attribute, at least when people taking the inventory acknowledge they have goals. When we combine expectations or goals that are based on what a recognized recovery program (AA) endorses with a universally accepted code of values and human goals (the self-actualization argument), the validity of the inventory is strengthened.

It's important to note that the Promises Checklist can be used in ongoing counseling with the patient, not just as a periodic check on whether counseling is working. The checklist, through the presentation of the topics of the Promises, becomes the vehicle through which to discuss this question: "Just what do you want in sobriety?" That question becomes critical in about the third month and then again in the third year of recovery, whether or not it is asked explicitly during treatment. It should be asked in treatment, if not for the reasons described above, then because we know what patients will come to want if they follow the Twelve Step program, and it is not what patients think we want for them when they first enter treatment. In the very least, the checklist provides a format for discussing issues such as the meaning of freedom and happiness. Tracking the changes in these concepts over time is often rewarding to both patient and counselor.

The Promises Checklist appears on page 74; another copy of the checklist, more suitable for sharing with patients, appears in appendix B. The patient workbook also includes the checklist.

On the Promises Checklist, the client indicates, perhaps once a month or as often as the client and counselor agree, to what extent he or she has been aware of the thirteen different feelings or circumstances (the topics of the Promises) in the past week. This checklist can prompt a discussion between counselor and patient of how recovery seems to be beneficial or problematic. This tool helps keep the main goals of recovery alive. If the checklist doesn't reveal progress, both the counselor and client should want to know why. Has new grief consumed the patient's energy? Is the person stuck in some

Promises Checklist

In the space provided, rate each feeling or circumstance on a scale of 1 to 5, based on how strong or weak your experience of it was in the past week.

  1 = a very weak sense or experience; none; or nearly none

  2 = some, but not much

  3 = a moderate amount, enough so you might say, "Yes, that's been happening."

  4 = more than a moderate amount, enough so you might say, "I've had a good experience of that this week."

  5 = a very strong experience, maybe a highlight of the week

1. Freedom   _____

2. Happiness   _____

3. Absence of regrets   _____

4. Serenity or peacefulness   _____

5. How much your experience benefits other people   _____

6. Absence of self-pity   _____

7. Interest in other people   _____

8. Absence of selfishness   _____

9. A more positive attitude about life   _____

10. Absence of fear of people   _____

11. Absence of fear of economic insecurity   _____

12. An ability to handle situations that used to be difficult   _____

13. Awareness of a Higher Power in your life   _____

pattern involving Denial, Insistence, or Passivity (DIP)? The checklist can uncover a number of issues and questions.

The checklist may prove particularly helpful in detecting grief. Chapter 6 described the behaviors and feelings of grief as if they could be directly seen or witnessed, but sometimes such things are only indirectly observed. Feelings of anger may be evidenced in items 4, 7, 9, and 12 of the checklist; feelings of depression in items 2, 3, 6, and 11. Counselors may devise their own methods of interpreting the checklist, but any interpretation should be done only with the joint participation of the patient. The checklist is not intended to be a diagnostic tool that roots out unseen issues, but rather is a record of the positive outcomes of recovery progress. The presence of grief, especially, is not seen as a weakness or liability in the patient but as a symptom of feelings that may characterize the impending end of the Push phase. When grief and bereavement occur in the Pull phase, they may be marked by a sense of appreciation for that which has been lost, with an absence of self-pity (item 6), and with renewed interest in life (item 9). In other words, it's expected that people in the Pull phase will have different responses to these items, and not necessarily higher scores on all of them, than people in the Push phase. Regret (item 3), for example, may be strongly present at the same time that serenity also appears and worry about financial insecurity is absent. Interpreting this checklist rests on some dialogue with the person, rather than a set of norms standardized on a different group.

Now is a good time to stop and fill out the Promises Checklist as it applies to your own life. After doing so, identify the items that received your strongest marks. If any were marked 5, how "circumstantial" was it; that is, due to a specific event last week? If it's not circumstantial, does it mean that you've experienced that item in a continuous way for quite a while and that it is now something you'd consider an enduring aspect in your life? Now identify the items that received your lowest marks (1s or 2s). How circumstantial are those feelings? Do you talk to anybody about them?

As may now be clear, the checklist invites discussion because it does not seek out "explanations" for the ratings: those are left for the patient to offer verbally, if asked. It does not probe into hypothetical scenarios but can provide grist for the mill of such discussion. To borrow an example from solution-focused therapy, the counselor might ask a version of the "miracle question": "What else in your life would change if all of those Promises came true next week? Who would notice?"[1]

The checklist takes only a few minutes to complete, can be done individually or as part of a group activity. It says to the patient, "Somebody cares what kind of experiences you're having." If people ask why it is called a "Promises" checklist, tell them, "because a well-known book says that these things can start happening if people take certain suggestions, which we'll be talking about." Then open the Big Book (third edition) to page 83 and read the passage that introduced this chapter. Comment on what the word "painstaking" might mean.[2]

For individuals who want no part of treatment or sobriety, who believe that alcohol and other drugs were more helpful than harmful, ask them to make a thirteen-item list of "promises" that their drug of choice made to them; that is, the thirteen best payoffs for continuing to use chemicals. Then compare their list with the Promises Checklist. The two lists will probably have a lot in common (freedom, absence of regret, ability to handle new situations). Point out that sobriety and recovery do not mean one has to give up seeking one's dreams, but that drug use has a somewhat different price than abstinence and recovery. The addiction developed in the first place because the person found a temporary payoff through alcohol or other drug use. Some people can find this payoff (addicts) while others can't (nonaddicts). The payoff for addiction, however, doesn't last and has to be chemically prompted until the supply of chemicals runs out or until other people must manage their lives for them. Getting the Promises to come true through sobriety at first seems an impossibly ridiculous idea, but that's *why* they are *promises*, made to those who need reassurance that life doesn't dead-end when they do Step 1. If the notion of abstinence and recovery were not ridiculous ideas to most addicts, they would not need promises or any other help to get sober.

Eventually, many addicted people see treatment as "the lesser of two evils," the alternative being some crisis of larger proportions. *It takes a crisis to get people into treatment for their addictions.* That is why structured intervention (a rehearsed and highly organized confrontation by meaningful others) is so effective: it precipitates a controlled crisis, which is preferable over an uncontrolled one. Treatment itself is a crisis for patients. Patients need and deserve some reassurance that their situation will "get better," something more than "this will pass; just hold on and be patient." The first time they complete the Promises Checklist, they may snicker in disbelief that such things would happen. However, the checklist doesn't ask them to *believe* it: it only asks clients to acknowledge their recent experiences. Belief *follows* experience. Remember the quote from the Big Book: "[W]e will be amazed before we are half way through." Every patient entering a treatment program is entitled to some of that amazement, as are his or her counselors. The snickering can change to appreciative laughter.

8

THE COMPONENTS
OF SELF-ESTEEM

Maslow's hierarchy (see figure 5, page 47) presents self-esteem as the stage of need preceding self-expression. Some consider self-esteem a recovery goal in itself and, thereby, worthy of analysis. However, seen as a stepping-stone to self-expression, it becomes the last building block in the construction of a fulfilling life. Related to self-esteem is the development of personal boundaries, which become clearer at this level. In recovery, these issues of esteem and boundaries are critical to the final goals of self-actualizing.

The topic of self-esteem has been encountered several times already in this book. Chapter 3, figure 3, discussed the onset of the Pull phase of recovery at point P2, which lies just below the level of self-esteem. Chapter 4 noted that not only does the AAA process contribute to self-esteem, but it also takes some self-esteem to progress into the second and third cycles (Steps 5–9 and 10–12). Finally, self-esteem plays a role in Promises 2, 3, 4, 6, 8, 9, 10, and 11, as listed on page 71. Now it's time to expand on what we've learned about self-esteem so far. In this chapter, we'll explore the relationship of self-esteem to confidence, sense of self-worth, boundaries, responsibility, creativity, identity, dependence, actualization, and the Promises. In other words, it all starts coming together here.

The terms self-esteem, self-confidence, and self-worth all

refer to a sense of self-valuing. The three terms are, however, best understood as related in a particular conceptual way, as shown in table 4.

In this scheme, self-esteem is the broadest term, encompassing both self-worth and self-confidence. A simple formula captures the idea:

Self-Esteem = Self-Confidence + Self-Worth

Self-worth is separated from self-confidence in terms of what it feels like and especially in terms of where it comes from—its etiology.

TABLE 4

Self-Esteem =

Self-Confidence	+	Self-Worth
Ability to do things		Ability to be
Learning through doing		Becoming through nurturing
Action-based		Being-based
Loss gives rise to guilt		Loss gives rise to shame

Self-confidence, according to table 4, consists of a set of beliefs and expectations people have about their ability to accomplish tasks of value, such as fixing the toaster, typing a letter, getting an "A" on the next exam, or running a hundred yards in ten seconds. Self-worth, however, refers to people's concurrent and separate set of beliefs about whether they are worthy of the applause that may come with any accomplishment, whether they are basically okay if the task isn't completed, or whether they're lovable for who they are rather than for what they can or cannot do.

Self-worth, rather than self-confidence, is voiced as a paramount concern in the recovery of addicted people and adult children from drug-affected families. For example, Cermak (1986) notes the change in level of self-esteem that comes with stage 4 in the recovery process from codependence:

> During this stage, chemical dependents and codependents weave a belief system, which legitimizes self-acceptance. Self-worth stops being something that must be earned, moment-by-moment, through one's accomplishments or through relationship with others. (pp. 75–76)

The problem, as identified by Cermak, is that so many dependents and codependents try to establish self-esteem by earning it. According to table 4, only part of self-esteem—namely, self-confidence—can be "earned." The other part, self-worth, has to be "received" as a loving gift from others, through nurturing, until the person feels worthy. Then self-esteem has two balancing components, the earned and the given.

Here's an example to illustrate the important differences between self-confidence and self-worth. Suppose Billy, a precocious seven-year-old, is severely injured in an accident and loses an arm and both legs. Before the accident, he had shown competence in doing things like throwing a baseball, riding his bike, cleaning his room, and playing computer games. Now, all of those abilities are compromised, perhaps absent entirely. If Billy's self-esteem depends entirely on his abilities to do things, then it will be shattered. If, however, his family and friends have nourished in him a sense of self-worth independent of these abilities and if he still can believe that he has a place on this planet just because he showed up here, then his self-esteem may understandably falter but not entirely collapse.

By far, most addicts and codependents in recovery have much more of their self-esteem based upon self-confidence than upon self-worth. When their self-confidence is weakened (by their inability to control their addiction), their self-esteem rides only on a fragile self-worth, which may be reduced to the barest minimum when they work Step 1 of a recovery program.

Self-esteem grows out of relationships with others and these relationships fall into two different types, or sets. One set of relationships supports what the person can do. A second set of relationships gives the person the support and love to do it. If one doesn't have both kinds of relationships, recovery is lessened and some of the Promises simply won't materialize. These two sets are called W (for work) and L (for love) in figure 6.

Figure 6 depicts a line, or scale, on which relationships with others, from strangers to our closest loved ones, can be charted for a particular moment in time. The part of the line labeled "Friends" is easy to understand. We feel good when we're around these people. Yet the level of these friendships vary. Some friendships are only slightly more meaningful than the interactions that occur with "companions," who are people with whom we share activities. The scale suggests giving a weight of 50 to such friendships. Farther to the right are more meaningful friendships and farther still to the right are relationships with significant others (spouses, mates, partners). The scale suggests giving a weight of 100 or more to each of these. On the far right end of the scale are the relationships with people in the person's family of origin. The scale suggests a weight of 1,000 for each of these. These weights would not necessarily remain constant throughout recovery.

Several important ideas are captured in figure 6, which is heavily based on the ideas of Gorski (1985). First, a relationship with a significant other or with someone from one's family of origin packs considerably more weight, or meaning, than a relationship with a casual acquaintance. Although the numbers on

FIGURE 6

The Relationship Scale

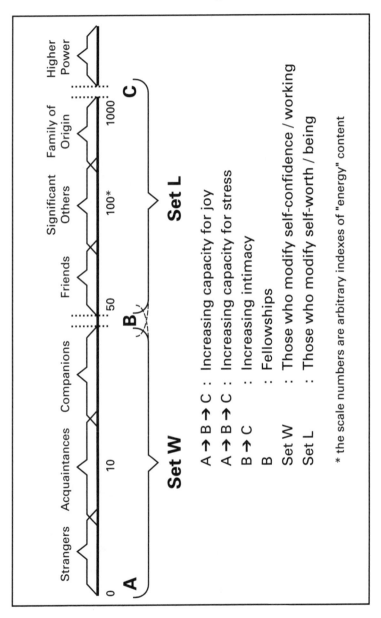

Strangers | Acquaintances | Companions | Friends | Significant Others | Family of Origin | Higher Power

0 10 50 100* 1000

Set W **Set L**

A **B** **C**

A → B → C : Increasing capacity for joy
A → B → C : Increasing capacity for stress
B → C : Increasing intimacy
B : Fellowships
Set W : Those who modify self-confidence / working
Set L : Those who modify self-worth / being

* the scale numbers are arbitrary indexes of "energy" content

the scale are arbitrary, their meaning is clear: the weight of a relationship reflects that relationship's capacity to produce both stress and joy in the person. Thus, the relationships capable of creating the greatest happiness are the very ones most capable of provoking the greatest stress. This underlies the popular sentiment "You only hurt the ones you love."

Second, when a relationship moves up or down the scale and to a different category, that movement requires or produces energy. This is the same idea as electrons changing orbits and energy levels, but applied to a human scale. As our relationships evolve, we experience constantly changing capacities for stress, joy, and levels of energy.

In figure 6, set L (the portion to the right of point B) is a scale of intimacy; these relationships offer the opportunity to fully express ourselves knowingly and with acceptance. The scale suggests that our most intimate relationships, those packed with greatest capacity for both stress and joy, are those with our family of origin. The legend in figure 6 indicates that in set W (left of point B), the idea of intimacy doesn't apply and, further, at this point there is a break in the continuity of the scale. Indeed, what happens at this point on the person's scale of relationships may determine whether a person moves into a self-actualizing life. One of the main keys to successful recovery and the transition from Push to Pull orientation occurs in the dynamics at point B.

To illustrate the crucial difference between the categories of "Companions" (the category to the left of point B) and "Friends" (the category to the right), consider the case of Chris, who has a friend named Tom. One evening, Chris decides she wants to go see a play, which is having its last showing that night, and she doesn't want to go alone. So, Chris calls Tom and asks if he would like to go with her. Tom says he really would like to see the performance but has to work that night. He suggests Chris call Trudy, a woman Chris met about three weeks ago at Tom's party.

Use figure 6 to locate Chris's relationships with Tom and Trudy at this point in the scenario. On Chris's scale, Tom is probably in the middle of the "Friends" category, at about 70. Chris and Tom are good buddies without a romantic or exclusive relationship. Trudy, on the other hand, is on Chris's scale somewhere in the "Acquaintance" category: Chris recalls meeting Trudy and exchanging a few words about common interests, so Trudy is not a complete stranger. But if Chris now contacts Trudy and they agree to go to the play, Trudy becomes a "Companion" on Chris's scale. Unlike friends, companions are people who get together only for sharing some activity. When the activity ends, so does their relationship. This may be what happens with Chris and Trudy after the play.

The relationship between Chris and Tom, however, is indeed a friendship if the following criterion (among others) is met: Tom or Chris decide to see each other even when there is no planned activity. Companionships are centered on activities; friendships are centered on people. Of course, friends do things together, but they don't *have* to.

In early Push phase recovery, many people remark, "I don't see any of my friends now that I've stopped drinking." This is an example of the confusion between friends and companions. The people with whom a person shared *only* the activity of drinking were not and are not friends, but rather companions. When the activity that brought them together ceases, so does the companionship. With friends, the activity never makes a critical difference in the relationship. So when a person stops drinking and using, the relationships "cemented" by those activities often end and reveal themselves as companionships rather than friendships. In recovery, both a new set of companions and friends invariably emerge. This can produce new stress and joy.

Often the difference between these two types of relationships contributes a lot of confusion and turmoil. A touchy situation exists when you are my friend, but I am your companion. I care about you, whatever we are doing, but you care more about what we are doing than about me. We are set up for resentments: I'll resent feeling I have to do things to keep you as a friend, and you'll resent me wanting to chat and spend idle time together. This may sound familiar. It is the dilemma of dating and trying to coordinate mutual feelings, which may turn out not to be mutual.

Intimate relationships, as described above, exist only with friends, significant others, or people from one's family of origin—at levels of personal involvement in figure 6 to the right of point B. This point on the relationship scale is very special; all societies have special customs or institutions for regulating, facilitating, or ritualizing the transitions relationships undergo when they move from categories left of point B to categories on the right. In the United States, some of these institutions may be fraternal groups; others simply call themselves fellowships. Alcoholics Anonymous, as an organization or fellowship, is at point B. The purpose of AA meetings is to carry the message to (or get a message from) alcoholics who still suffer. (That is the *group's* purpose; the individual's purpose is to stay sober.) For those purposes, all of the people at a meeting are companions, sharing the activity of recovery where "principles before personalities" is a central theme of the activity. Out of the companionship within AA, or any fellowship, may grow friendships characterized by a focus on the personality, on the person, rather than on the activities of the fellowship. The relationship between an AA member and his or her sponsor has elements of both companionship and friendship and is special in that regard. Such relationships usually are unstable. Any relationship at the edge or border of two categories produces tension. Those who have tried to remain close friends with a former sweetheart or spouse know the tensions involved.

Referring back to table 4 (page 80) and then to figure 6 (page 83), we see that self-confidence is (or should be) a result of successful interaction in relationships with people in set W. This means that self-confidence in one's abilities to *do* things does *not* result from successful interaction with intimate friends or family, but rather from interactions with strangers, acquaintances, and companions—those relationships in which some form of work or "doing" is shared. This goes beyond the trivial observation that most people don't earn their livings at home working for friends and family. It is at the heart of what Anthony Storr sees as critical in developing a sense of Self apart from intimate others. Storr says:

> All human beings need interests as well as relationships; all are geared toward the impersonal as well as toward the personal. . . . The happiest lives are probably those in which neither interpersonal relationships nor impersonal interests are idealized as the only way to salvation. (1988, 202)

In terms of table 4 and figure 6, everyone needs interests and abilities that are not directly tied to the fates of close relationships. Everyone needs some autonomy, apart from being a good friend. Everyone needs things to do besides talk, listen, and touch, and to have confidence in their ability to make a place in the world of work and play among people who won't necessarily love or even know them.

Storr (1988) argues that the most important moments of the self-actualizing creative person's life are those in which the person is alone and unconnected to others. Storr studied

Maslow and quotes a portion of the following passage in which Maslow is writing on the creative attitude:

> *Very* important here is our lessened awareness of other people, of their ties to us and ours to them, of obligations, duties, fears, hopes, etc. We become much more free of other people, which in turn, means that we become much more ourselves, our Real Selves, our authentic selves, our real identity.

> This is so because *the* greatest cause of our alienation from our real selves is our neurotic involvements with other people, the historical hangovers from childhood, the irrational transference, in which past and present are confused, and in which the adult acts like a child. (Maslow 1971, 62)

The last paragraph sounds like something one might find in a current treatise on adult children of alcoholics, yet Maslow wrote it more than thirty years ago. Storr (1988) went on to argue that Maslow's attitude was very different from that of the object-relations theorists "who tend to assume that the meaning of life is invariably bound up with interpersonal relationships" (p. 201). Self-actualization demands a separate Self to actualize. Many writers, including Larsen (1985), may overemphasize the centrality of rebuilding intimate relationships, neglecting the importance of companionships because they are interested in examining self-worth more than self-confidence.

The nurturing of *self-worth* requires precisely those kinds of intimate relationships that are of little use in building self-confidence. Set L in figure 6 consists of relationships that help people feel unmistakably that they're valued and loved for reasons other than their abilities, skills, or talents. This nurturing arises from relationships that become more unconditional as they move from left to right on the scale.

Nurturing is one means of satisfying the need for love and

belonging, which is level 3 in Maslow's hierarchy of needs. Nurturing means sharing power and resources: people develop a sense of belonging to a place or in a group when they feel a sense of being able to affect things there or feel welcome to use the resources there. When people feel excluded ("I just don't fit in here; this isn't my kind of place"), it is often because they believe they don't have access to adequate resources (legal, family, financial), no power to influence their situation. So, they move elsewhere in search of belonging and caring.

However, when people are nurtured, their self-worth deepens. When children are nurtured, their resiliency deepens. They learn how to enlist the help of others, especially adults, because they feel they have access to those human resources. Nurtured people then have the permission and the opportunity to *be caring*, which is just as much a part of Maslow's level 3 needs as *being cared about* is. The next level of the pyramid, self-esteem, rests heavily upon this sense that "I am a caring person," and gets incorporated into the person's self-worth. In this way, the nurturing at level 3 in Maslow's hierarchy sets the stage for the possibility of adequate self-esteem at the next level.

The only way an adequate sense of self-worth develops is through people who provide nurturing as an unconditional gift. If one's family of origin did not nurture that sense of self-worth (which is what families are supposed to do), one will look for it at the next level down, among significant others, in the family that one creates. If it is not found there, one may seek where it cannot be found—among companions and acquaintances. At this level of relating, self-esteem then rests entirely upon self-confidence or upon a self-worth that has to be earned, like a salary. In that case, one has a role and a job at the expense of a Self.

Note that in table 4, guilt is associated with loss of self-confidence, whereas shame refers to loss of self-worth. Guilt refers to the feelings one has about some *act* that was or was not done, while shame refers to feelings about the inadequacy of *Self*, independent of specific behaviors. The sense of shame is much harder to rectify, because the antidote to guilt is making amends and improving behavior, whereas the antidote to shame is *acceptance by others*. Through our own acts we can handle guilt, but it takes nurturing, acceptance, and support from others to heal shame.

In Alcoholics Anonymous, guilt is relieved (not removed) through Steps 8 and 9, which involve Action. On the other hand, shame is relieved through Asking in Steps 6 and 7 for removal of character defects, which may be the source of the shame. Steps 8 and 9 entail rectifying situations out of conscience (or healthy guilt); recognition of this newfound conscience may actually further the relief from shame begun in Steps 6 and 7.

Here, then, is the meat of the previously stated hypothesis: the person in recovery, moving in the direction of enhanced self-actualization, needs a variety of relationships, from both ends of the scale in figure 6, in order for healthy self-esteem to be realized. Further, some of the Promises may be fulfilled by relationships outside of intimate ones, while others will be realized only with the nurturing of friends, loved ones, and fellowship. Self-esteem will come partly as a gift, unearned, while part has to come through effort, trial, and courage. This has been AA's message all along, verified here with independent consideration of self-actualization models.

At this point a reminder is needed: self-esteem doesn't develop magically. The process of Admit, Ask, Act (AAA) is still at work here. Even though self-worth comes as a gift from others, the recovering person still has to seek it out, ask for it, and show up to receive it. Self-responsibility is a prerequisite to self-esteem, and that responsibility is first felt in the Push phase. Self-esteem builds later, upon successful working of the Twelve Steps in fellowship.

If people have been in recovery for months or years and have not yet found a way to get their needs for love and belonging met, then their self-esteem, at the next level in the hierarchy, is probably fragile. If their self-esteem is fragile, they have a hard time maintaining personal boundaries. This means they can't discriminate their business from someone else's, can't fend off intrusions into their personal space, whether it is physical intrusion ("Stop that, please don't poke at me like that") or mental ("Please don't interrupt; let me finish what I was saying") or spiritual ("No, that's not what I believe—you are jumping to conclusions about me").

People in recovery will start rebuilding personal boundaries at the second level (safety and security) in the hierarchy when they begin exercising their sense of confidence and worth. Then boundaries are "tested." At this point, they may be accused of being "touchy," "aloof," or "selfish," while they're really gaining the ability to say, "This far and no further" when others make unreasonable requests. These individuals no longer invest their self-esteem only in their ability to help or protect others; no longer do they need to control a crisis single-handedly or do things that used to cause them resentment. They are taking on more of the characteristics of self-actualized people discussed in chapter 5, including the ability to take good care of themselves. They are also now seeking out and finding others who, like themselves, are able to be independent but not isolated, able to share feelings without having to "fix" things, and able to laugh about the things that used to trigger anxiety and self-doubt. They are abiding in a sense of gratitude for the manifestation of the Promises.

They have a set of values, the Source of which is trusted beyond all other things.

—*//*—

9

CONCLUSION

As people progress in recovery, eventually they will no longer need counselors. They may seek advice (they still Ask a lot), excel at Admitting when things are what they are, and take Action when needed. Although this may require seeing a counselor from time to time, the recovering persons are now taking responsibility for seeking out certain people. Nobody is so healthy that they do not need a physician on occasion, and no recovering person can manage all aspects of recovery without input and output to others. As Alcoholics Anonymous asserts, "We claim progress rather than perfection." The return of Denial, Insistence, and Passivity is still possible but is no longer linked to their addictions. People are being Pulled toward something they sense as a destiny, not just a destination. For someone in early recovery, especially someone just entering his or her own Pull phase, meeting another person who is at this level of self-actualizing can be enormously rewarding. The counselor should be at this level, part of the Pull on the recovering person.

We have seen that Maslow's level 3 (love and belonging) sets the stage for self-esteem. Love and belonging can mean many things to different people, but it should include the solutions to the needs for being cared about and *also having something or someone to care about.* People, according to Maslow, have a natural need to express care as well as receive it. One can't very well believe that he really belongs to a group if he cares about none of the other group members. The group could be a family, fellowship, platoon, or culture. To establish a sense of belonging, one must feel both cared about and caring. When a patient returns from his or her first AA meeting and says something such as, "I just don't belong there," the counselor may well ask, not sarcastically, "Where do you belong?" A patient who replies, "Nowhere," is revealing a lot about his or her unmet needs. People in the early Push phase may feel they are not cared about and/or may believe they care about no one else. Such people have self-esteem that is fragile, which may show up as excessive grandiosity or as abject resignation and fear. Rebuilding starts from the ground up, first with physiological concerns (do the individuals have what they consider an ugliness, linked to health?), then on to safety and security (where do you feel safe?), care and belonging (if you could be a part of any group at all, what would that be?). In other words, we can't do self-esteem building without looking at the underlying levels of unmet needs. Programs for youth, for example, that purport to build self-confidence through wilderness adventures have learned that first, not later, one has to have a group of youth that has a common spirit and that they are well fed and feel safe within the group.

Finally, a comment about what may be the most interesting and most misunderstood level, self-expression at the top of the pyramid. Self-expression does not mean standing on a street corner spouting one's theory of alien invasion. That is freedom of speech. Self-expression goes further, and sober self-expression goes further yet. Self-expression means doing what feels right, without alarm, without coercion, voluntarily, with full interest and passion. It doesn't mean selfish self-preoccupation. Rather, in self-expression, a purpose or a cause lies at the heart of the effort, which extends beyond the individual's immediate interest. When truly self-actualizing people are "doing their thing," others take note with appreciation, curiosity, and admiration. These individuals express themselves reliably, that is, not haphazardly, and with style. Your heroes and heroines are doing it. It is what we hope our children will continue to do long after they are no longer children.

We are all compelled to discover and follow our bliss. People who are addicted to alcohol or other drugs found the wrong Self emerging from a bottle or needle. Recovery means finding the right one. For that, we need help. We find our bliss in the Pull of things.

It would be a mistake for people to believe that once their needs are met at Maslow's first four levels, they can then spend all of their time "doing their own thing." People have to work at reinforcing the lower levels: eat, sleep, lock the doors, express care, show up at family gatherings, and try our skills at new tasks. Self-actualization is a continuous process; it is more like a long spiral of overlapping circles than a linear ladder that we climb toward an ever-increasing realization of our potential.

Often overlooked in discussions of Maslow's theory is the way people help each other. People who get their needs met help others get theirs. The success of fellowships like Alcoholics Anonymous and other Twelve Step programs relies on this. One usually chooses a sponsor who is "higher" on the pyramid of activity than oneself. In some sense, it is possible to be Pulled not only forward, but up.

At the level of self-expression, we find people doing things they believe are meaningful and important. They love their work. They are not "alone in a cave" busily shaping a private world of solitary enjoyments. Instead, they are in contact with others who are doing similar things, for similar reasons. They often have apprentices; they often teach. In addition, they usually are sought out for counsel. They do what they do but *they don't have to*. They could quit and pursue something else. The freedom and joy (and stress) are revealed in the continuing fulfillment of the Promises in their lives. Recovering people should expect and strive for no less than any other human.

This, then, is the simple definition of recovery: *the recovery of the self-actualizing potential that is lost in active addiction.* With the Steps and the AAA cycles, with the monitoring of the Promises, with the resolution of loss and grief, people in recovery can have powerful advantages to help themselves and others in the actualization of a spiritual awakening that reshapes their world. *Assessing recovery then means attending to the process of AAA, to the resolution of natural problems like grief, to the arrival and fostering of the Promises, and to the successful attainment of need satisfaction at higher and higher levels in Maslow's pyramid. There is a hierarchy of processes and of results in recovery, not just an assortment of arbitrarily related events.*

Counselors and helpers who get people started through treatment will hopefully be able to say:

> This is the road, this is your burden, this is your map, and there is the destination. And here are those traveling with you; here in this book are some who have gone before; here are some things to expect to find and experience along the way. I'll accompany you for a while, and help you read the map. Anytime you want, you can ask, "Where are we, what's going on?" and I'll tell you as best as I can. My job is not just to help you stay on the path but to see how you're doing and especially to make it worth your while to take this trip. Let's see what you've got in your pack there, and let's do some tests on your ability to start going ahead. Every once in a while the road gets steep, everybody groans, and some come to a stop and head back the way they came. So I'll ask how things are going, how you're feeling, what's been added to

your pack or taken out. And every once in a while, I'll send a note out asking where you are and how you're doing.

And the person, patient, or journeyer might then say, "Sounds good to me. Let's go."

—*//*—

APPENDIX A

The AAA Profile

Date _____

For each item below, indicate the extent to which you agree or disagree with the statement. Use the following scale:

5 = This statement applies to me all the time.

4 = This statement applies to me much of the time.

3 = This statement sometimes applies to me.

2 = This statement rarely applies to me.

1 = This statement never applies to me.

There are no right and wrong answers in this exercise. Answer as honestly as possible how these statements apply or do not apply to you. Put your response (one number from above) in the blank following each statement.

1. I am a procrastinator; I put things off. _____

2. I admit when I am wrong. _____

3. I prefer to do things without help. _____

4. When I know what needs to be done, I do it. _____

5. I am open to suggestions. _____

6. I know when I'm not happy, but I don't talk about it. _____

7. It is hard for me to ask for things. _____

8. Friends say that I am a "doer." _____

9. I do not like keeping secrets. _____

10. I am more of a thinker than a doer. _____

11. It takes a lot of evidence before I see
    something about myself I hadn't seen before.   _____

12. I am willing to do things differently than I
    usually do them.   _____

13. I am enjoying life.   _____

Scoring the AAA Profile

A. Add the numbers recorded for items **2 and 9:**   _____

B. Add the numbers recorded for items **6 and 11:**   _____

C. Subtract B from A: _____
   (If B is larger than A, put a negative sign in front of this result.)

D. Add the numbers recorded for items **5 and 12:**   _____

E. Add the numbers recorded for items **3 and 7:**   _____

F. Subtract E from D: _____
   (If E is larger than D, put a negative sign in front of this result.)

G. Add the numbers recorded for items **4 and 8:**   _____

H. Add the numbers recorded for items **1 and 10:**   _____

I. Subtract H from G: _____
   (If H is larger than G, put a negative sign in front of this result.)

   The ADMIT index is C: _____

   The ASK index is F: _____

   The ACT index is I: _____

**Note: Each index score can range from lowest
to highest as follows:**

-8, -7, -6, -5, -4, -3, -2, -1, 0, 1, 2, 3, 4, 5, 6, 7, 8
(low   high)

Draw a circle around the largest number (C, F, or I)

This is the person's strongest element in the AAA process:

———————

■

Draw a square around the smallest number (C, F, or I)

This is the person's weakest element in the AAA process:

———————

■

An index lower than -3 indicates a problem area.

An index between 1 and 3 indicates a realistic strength.

An index higher than 5 probably is wishful thinking or compliance.

■

List the number entered for item 13 _____ .

Subtract the number entered for item 6 _____ .

If the result is 3 or less, talk about item 13 first, before going over the rest of the profile.

APPENDIX B

Promises Checklist

Date _____

In the space provided, rate each feeling or circumstance on a scale of 1 to 5, based on how strong or weak your experience of it was in the past week.

1 = a very weak sense or experience; none; or nearly none

2 = some, but not much

3 = a moderate amount, enough so you might say,
    "Yes, that's been happening."

4 = more than a moderate amount, enough so you might say, "I've had a good experience of that this week."

5 = a very strong experience, maybe a highlight of the week

1. Freedom _____

2. Happiness _____

3. Absence of regrets _____

4. Serenity or peacefulness _____

5. How much your experience benefits other people _____

6. Absence of self-pity _____

7. Interest in other people _____

8. Absence of selfishness _____

9. A more positive attitude about life _____

10. Absence of fear of people _____

11. Absence of fear of economic insecurity _____

12. An ability to handle situations that used to be difficult _____

13. Awareness of a Higher Power in your life _____

NOTES

Introduction

1. Coping skills, in my opinion, are a greatly overrated response to the problem of relapse. In Gorski's (1989) model of the relapse dynamic, for example, coping skills as tools of recovery persist even into stage 6, the maintenance stage *following* the late recovery stage. Presumably, coping skills (like progressive relaxation) are taught to help people cope with stress and other risk factors. But in late-stage recovery, almost by definition, the number of risk factors and stressors that could threaten sobriety should be so significantly reduced that the coping skills have outlived their necessity. The person who plays with matches needs a fire extinguisher, but the person who doesn't just needs the number of the fire department. We seriously underestimate the ability of people with long-term sobriety to manage their own affairs and to take guidance from their own Higher Power to handle the rest of it. As we'll see in chapter 3, one feature of recovery in the Pull phase is that the person knowingly extends his or her behavior into situations (such as relationships and new careers and parenting) that used to be "risky business"; the person no longer plays it so safe that sobriety is just an exercise in avoiding all risks, taking no chances, and attending workshops on what can go wrong if caution is not taken. At some point, the recovering person "graduates" into being a person who knows which risks to take and which ones to avoid. This is not to say that I advocate "flirting with danger," especially for people in the earlier Push phase. Nor am I suggesting anyone "flirt with safety," a concept yet to be recognized as a hallmark of alcoholic unpreparedness for abstinence. Nor am I saying there is any point in the future of a recovering person where he or she is assured immunity to relapse (to find out what I *am* suggesting, read chapter 3).

Chapter 1: Recovery: By What Criteria?

1. With regard to table 1, it is evident there is *some* consensus among both laypersons and professionals concerning criteria for recovery in the first year of abstinence. There is certainly nothing wrong with using, say, the first six criteria listed in table 1 as recovery criteria. After all, these first six items received endorsement by 55 percent of the conference group. One could then proceed, in the fashion of the *DSM-IV* for criteria for any syndrome of clinical interest, to list these six criteria and agree that, say, adequate progress in any four of these represents satisfactory recovery. These are legitimate *treatment* goals. But these criteria are insufficient as *recovery* criteria because of what would be left out. Number 8, long-term goals, would not be there, nor would number 10, self-esteem, nor number 12, spiritual connection. Especially number 14, referring to enjoyment of life and sense of well-being, would be absent. On page 132 of *Alcoholics Anonymous* (3d ed.) is a sentence that includes the phrase "we absolutely insist," the only place in the whole Big Book where I can find the authors insisting on something rather than making a suggestion. The entire sentence reads, "We absolutely insist on enjoying life." It is written in the context of trying not to give an impression to the newcomer that alcoholics in recovery are a "glum lot." I think the insistence on enjoying life in recovery is one worth repeating and including in recovery criteria. I further believe that if some of the elements of self-esteem, spiritual connection, and enjoyment of life are not *expected* outcomes by counselors, they might not appear in patients for just that reason. The first six criteria, except number 5, are means to ends. The ends themselves are things like numbers 10, 12, and 14, which are potential experiences of the patient. Recovering people need positive experiences and cannot wait a year to get them. The rest of the book, then, presents ideas on how to incorporate these things into recovery criteria.

Chapter 3: The Push and Pull of Recovery

1. The Pull phase should not be confused with Larsen's Stage II recovery. In Larsen's book (1985), in an appended chapter at the end, there are some comments made by people in Stage II about what Stage II is like, and most follow Larsen's philosophy that "learning to make relationships work is at the core of full recovery" (p.15). But of the fifty-two comments in that section, only three mention anything like happiness, enjoyment of life, freedom, or indeed any positive markers of recovery other than having a more successful relationship with someone. But what is a successful relationship if it does not bring enjoyment or happiness or fulfillment? So "learning to make relationships work" is just another task faced by people who haven't had many, and Stage II relationship building doesn't get talked about as a "payoff," but rather as a job. For reasons developed later in this book, the Pull phase encompasses more than successful relationships: it includes the development of the Self, and that endeavor always includes, but transcends, significant others.

2. I wish to thank Mike Doran for the following analogy of the differences between the Push and the Pull phases of recovery: Imagine driving in your new car down a long road that leads to a hill, over the top of which is a fabled "land-of-plenty." The road has many potholes and ruts, and no turnouts. Either one can drive very slowly, trying to avoid all the holes and problem spots, focusing on how far one has come from the last service station, or one can keep an eye on the road ahead, trying for the surest route rather than the smoothest ride. In the first case (Push phase), one worries about whether the car can take the jolts and what happens if one gets stuck or runs out of gas; in the second case (Pull), one trusts the car (sobriety) and knows there is a service station just beyond the top of the hill. Recovery involves both kinds of driving.

Chapter 5: Self-Actualization

1. Some examples of self-actualizing people may be of help here. Maslow himself considered people like Abraham Lincoln, Albert Einstein, William James, and Henry David Thoreau, among many others, to be familiar examples of what he was talking about. As with these individuals, self-actualizing people are not "perfect" people: each of them had human flaws. Nor do actualizing people have to be famous or rich: I personally know several who are neither, nor do they care to be. Chances are high that the reader's own personal heroes are examples of self-actualizing people, whether they are real or fictional, living or dead. Some of my heroes are Bill W., Charles Dickens, Mark Twain, Meryl Streep, to name a few who are more famous than the rest. They are noted for their creativity, good humor, courage of conviction, and for doing the best they are capable of doing in what they choose to do. They are people you'd like to spend time with. There are millions and millions, and, according to Maslow and me, you want to be one too.

2. The well-used and helpful acronym HALT has been offered by AA as a guide to prevent relapse: don't get Hungry, Angry, Lonely, or Tired, and especially don't let all four happen at the same time! Looking at this advice in terms of Maslow's model, hunger seems to be a main danger at the physiological base of the pyramid; anger can be seen as a response to threats to safety or security; loneliness can be viewed as a problem at the level of love and belonging; and tired may well be the result of trying too hard or too long to do the things you like to do at the level of self-expression. AA wisdom long ago captured the notions that Maslow's hierarchy put into a framework to describe not just recovery, but the human condition. For recovering people, unmet needs can trigger relapse if the person isn't able to Acknowledge those needs, Ask for help, and take Action.

Chapter 6: Grief

1. Psychopathic people do not experience what is being called grief here. Instead, they experience frustration and self-serving worry—what will I do now? In part, this is because of their lack of conscience; they have little regard for the value of things or people apart from how they can be of use to them. Grief is a reaction to the loss, or impending loss, of something important. To the psychopath, the only things of importance are those that can advance their needs for power and control; hence money is important, but honesty is not. Drugs are additionally important to the extent that they allowed even greater assertion, or covering up, of personal agendas, and psychopaths feel protective of their drugs in the same way that they might feel protective of a weapon. True criminal psychopathy—namely, full antisocial personality disorder with violence—warrants status as a co-occurring disorder when seen in combination with addiction to chemicals. People with this dual diagnosis have a very poor prognosis of entering the Pull phase, since (1) they cannot be honest with themselves (as warned in the AA Big Book, these are the ones who will fail in the suggested program); (2) they can experience pain, but pain seldom deters them from a course of action, and the psychopath does not cry when feeling pain; he strikes out at others; (3) psychopaths will go to great lengths to replace what was lost, feeling that they are "owed" when they surrender something, or lose it, and this happens without any change in their set of values, which remain totally self-centered. Psychopaths cannot be trusted, nor can they trust what they cannot see, and hence their Higher Power becomes themselves alone. This will get them into the Push phase, and perhaps keep them there a while, but the Pull phase does not happen. "There are such unfortunates, they seem to have been born that way."

2. Both the DIP cycle (discussed in chapter 4 as the opposite of the AAA cycle) and grief begin with denial. In both cases, denial may play the same role as a defense against pain. In grief, however, the denial is that something has been or is going to be lost; in the DIP context, the denial may be about anything. In the grief process, denial is often replaced by anger; in the DIP cycle, it is replaced by insistence. It is possible that people can be in both a grief process and a DIP cycle at the same time: they show an angry Insistence that they will "handle" the previously denied problem/loss in their own way. The Passivity of the DIP cycle may combine with the depression of the grief process. Such people are then hard to reach and hard to comfort, but the approach is the same: start with making it safe to experience the pain, a bit at a time, and have somebody available that they can seek out or ask questions of, and give them something relevant to do (like visit a grave, watch a movie, take a walk with someone). In short, use the AAA process as a response to the DIP aspect of the grief.

Chapter 7: The Promises

1. A counselor can also try the "I'll bet" technique with a patient whose reticence and withdrawal are revealing nothing about what he or she is feeling or thinking. The counselor fills out the checklist for the patient *in advance* of the patient's next appointment or meeting, and then says, "I'll bet your week has been like this . . ." and shows the patient the filled-out checklist. The patient may get angry (that the counselor did this), or point out the several wrong "guesses" the counselor made, or say, "How did you figure this out?" or may say, "Why did you rate me so low on item six? I don't have any self-pity." In any of these scenarios, the patient is now pointing at or talking about something relevant, which is one thing every recovering person must do. It is my hope that the counselor *sees it* as relevant. For patients who are not reticent and are eager to talk about events in their lives, the checklist can provide a focus for that, from time to time.

2. "Painstaking" can mean several things, all of which suggest the process of practicing the Steps is not easy—it is painful at first. Pain comes in many forms: the embarrassment of Step 1, the painful mystery of Step 2, the anxiety of Step 3, the barbs and nicks of Step 4, and so on. Patients are entitled to a reminder that this is not just "make work" to keep their minds busy and tormented but that there are payoffs, and the payoffs go beyond treatment compliance as answers to the question, asked in Reality Therapy, "What do you *really* want?"

—*//*—

REFERENCE LIST

AA World Services, Inc. 1952. *Twelve steps and twelve traditions.* New York: AA World Services, Inc.

——. 1976. *Alcoholics anonymous.* 3d ed. New York: AA World Services, Inc.

Alibrandi, L. A. 1978. The folk psychotherapy of Alcoholics Anonymous. In *Practical approaches to alcoholism psychotherapy,* edited by S. Zimberg, J. Wallace, and S. Blume. New York: Plenum Press.

American Psychiatric Association. 1994. *Diagnostic and statistical manual of mental disorders (DSM-IV).* 4th ed. Washington, D.C.: American Psychiatric Association.

Berenson, D. 1988. Alcoholics Anonymous: From surrender to transformation. *Utne Reader,* Nov./Dec.

Berg, Insoo Kim, and S. Miller. 2000. *Working with the problem drinker.* New York: W.W. Norton.

Blum, K., B. Elliot, J. Sexton, M. Trachtenberg, J. Dingler, D. Samuels, and S. Cataldie. 1987. Enkephalinase inhibition and precursor amino acid loading improves inpatient treatment of alcohol and polydrug abusers. *Bulletin Research* (report), Matrix Technologies, Houston, Tex. 19 pp.

Branden, N. 1983. *Honoring the self.* Chicago: Jeremy P. Tarcher, Inc.

Brown, S. 1985. *Treating the alcoholic.* New York: Wiley.

Cermak, T. 1986. *Diagnosis and treating co-dependence.* Minneapolis, Minn.: Johnson Institute.

Cloninger, C. R. 1987. Neurogenetic adaptive mechanisms in alcoholism. *Science* 236 (April 24): 410–16.

Coughlin, G., S. Anderson, and L. Kimbro. 1999. *Patient records and addiction treatment.* Port Townsend, Wash.: Lanstat Corp.

Daley, D., and A. Zuckoff. 1999. *Improving treatment compliance.* Center City, Minn.: Hazelden.

Gibbs, J., and J. Flanagan 1977. Prognostic indicators of alcoholism treatment outcome. *International Journal of the Addictions* 12:1097–1141.

Gorski, T. 1985. *Relationships and intimacy.* Hazel Crest, Ill.: Cenaps Corp. Audiotape (#167).

———. 1986. Relapse prevention planning. *Alcohol Health and Research World* 11, no. 1 (Fall).

———. 1989. *Passages through recovery.* Center City, Minn.: Hazelden.

Gorski, T., and M. Miller. 1986. *Staying sober.* Independence, Mo.: Independence Press.

Gravitz, H., and J. Bowden. 1987. *Recovery: A guide for adult children of alcoholics.* New York: Simon and Schuster.

Helgoe, R. 1986. Assessments of recovery: The positive aspects. Paper presented at the First Annual Merril Scott Symposium, Yakima, Wash.

Helgoe, R., P. Brown, J. Renaud, and L. Grant. 1985. *Comprehensive alcohol problem assessment manual.* Kirkland, Wash.: The Association of Alcoholism and Addiction Programs in Washington State.

Hoffman, A., and N. Estes. 1986. A tool for measuring body and behavioral experiences. *Alcohol Health and Research World* 11, no. 1 (Feb.).

———. 1987. Body and behavioral experiences in recovery from alcoholism. *Rehabilitation Nursing* 12 (4).

Hoffman, N. n.d. Fact sheet: AA and continuing sobriety. St. Paul, Minn.: CATOR Publications, Medical Education and Research Foundation.

James, William. 1961. *Psychology: The briefer course.* New York: Harper.

———. 1902. *The varieties of religious experience.* New York: The Modern Library.

Keen, S. 1983. *The passionate life: Stages of loving.* New York: Harper and Row.

Kellerman, J. L. 1992. *Grief: A basic reaction to alcoholism.* Center City, Minn.: Hazelden.

Kübler-Ross, E. 1969. *On death and dying.* New York: Macmillan.

Kurtz, E. 1979. *Not-God: A history of Alcoholics Anonymous.* Center City, Minn.: Hazelden.

Larsen, E. 1985. *Stage II recovery.* New York: Harper and Row.

Lettieri, D. 1986. Problems in predicting recovery from alcoholism. *Alcohol Health and Research World* 11 (1).

Maslow, A. 1954. *Motivation and personality.* New York: Harper and Row.

———. 1971. *The farther reaches of human nature.* New York: Penguin.

Massman, J. 1979. Normal recovery symptoms frequently experienced by the recovering alcoholic. In *Currents in Alcoholism Treatment and Rehabilitation*, Vol. 1. Edited by M. Galanter. N.p.: Grune and Stratton. Cited by Hoffman and Estes, 1987.

McDonald, P. C. 1996. *Grieving: A healing process.* Center City, Minn.: Hazelden.

Mee-Lee, D. 1988. An instrument for treatment progress and matching: The recovery attitude and treatment evaluator (RAATE). *Journal of Substance Abuse Treatment 5.*

Mee-Lee, D., G. Shulman, M. Fishman, D. Gastfriend, and J. Griffith, eds. 2001. *ASAM patient placement criteria for the treatment of substance-related disorders, second edition-revised (ASAM PPC-2R).* Chevy Chase, Md.: American Society of Addiction Medicine, Inc.

Middleton-Moz, J., and L. Dwinell. 1986. *After the tears: Grief and alcoholic family systems.* Edison, N.J.: Health Communications.

Miller, M., and T. Gorski. 1982. *Learning to live again.* 3d ed. Independence, Mo.: Independence Press.

Miller, W. R., and S. Rollnick. 1999. *Motivational interviewing: Preparing people to change addictive behavior.* New York: Guilford Press.

Patterson, C. 1985. *The therapeutic relationship: Foundation for an eclectic psychotherapy.* Pacific Grove, Calif.: Brooks-Cole.

Perrin, P., and W. Coleman. 1988. Is addiction really a misguided move toward wholeness? *Utne Reader,* Nov./Dec.

Reynolds, D. 1984a. *Constructive living.* Honolulu: University of Hawaii Press.

———. 1984b. *Playing ball on running water.* New York: William Morrow.

Rogers, R., C. McMillan, and M. Hill. 1988. *The Twelve Steps revisited.* Seattle, Wash.: Madrona Publications.

Royce, J. 1986. Addiction: A spiritual illness? Address to 32d International Institute on Prevention and Treatment of Alcoholism, June, in Budapest.

Sanchez-Craig, M. 1988. Procedures for assessing change after alcoholism treatment. In *Research strategies in alcoholism treatment assessment.* Binghampton, N.Y.: Haworth Press.

Schaef, A. 1988. Recovery as process. *Utne Reader,* Nov./Dec.

Storr, A. 1988. *Solitude: A return to the self.* New York: The Free Press.

Wallace, J. 1985. *Alcoholism: A new light on the disease.* Newport, R.I.: Edgehill Publications.

Wegscheider, S. 1981. *Another chance.* Palo Alto, Calif.: Science and Behavior Books.

Whitfield, C. 1985. *Alcoholism and spirituality.* Cleveland, Ohio: The Resource Group/Thomas Perrin.

Wubbolding, R. E. 1988. *Using reality therapy.* New York: Harper and Row.

ABOUT THE AUTHOR

Robert S. Helgoe, Ph.D., teaches in the human services program at Skagit Valley College, Mount Vernon, Washington. He is an adjunct staff member of the Skagit Recovery Center's intensive outpatient program and a treatment-outcomes consultant to Sundown M Ranch addictions treatment center at Selah, Washington. He currently serves on the Washington State Department of Health Chemical Dependency Professional Certification Advisory Committee and in 1999 received a Division of Alcohol and Substance Abuse award in recognition of his contributions to the field since 1980.